I hope you
this book.

Ella Mae

Come, Lord Jesus
A Study of Revelation

Mark Braaten

LITURGICAL PRESS
Collegeville, Minnesota

www.litpress.org

Cover design by David Manahan, O.S.B. Illustration courtesy of xBrandpictures.

1	2	3	4	5	6	7	8	9

Library of Congress Cataloging-in-Publication Data

Braaten, Mark.
   Come, Lord Jesus : a study of Revelation / Mark Braaten.
     p. cm.
   Includes bibliographical references.
   ISBN-13: 978-0-8146-3172-0 (alk. paper)
   ISBN-10: 0-8146-3172-X (alk. paper)
   1. Bible. N.T. Revelation—Textbooks. I. Title.

BS2825.55.B73 2007
228'.077—dc22   2006010336

Dedication
To Mom and Dad
for all the years of support, love, and guidance
To Amber, Christopher, and Cassaundra
for giving me a new depth of joy
And most of all to Karen
for walking with me, loving me, for deepening my life

Contents

Foreword

This project began as an attempt to find a book on Revelation for my father. My dad is a well-read lay member of the church. For years I've been passing on to him theology and biblical study books that I thought he would enjoy. Also for years he has asked me to find for him a good introduction to the book of Revelation. I had trouble finding such a book. I found many wonderful scholarly books on Revelation, with excellent interpretations and insights. But most of these books are written in a theological language that lay people do not have the training to understand. And yes, there are many popular books on Revelation. They are often easy to read, but too many of those books contain theology and interpretations that I find questionable and inaccurate. I was having trouble answering my dad's request for an introduction to Revelation.

I enrolled in the Doctor of Ministry program at Luther Seminary in St. Paul, Minnesota, in 1999 with the intent of studying Revelation and writing a study guide that my dad and others could use. I have spent a good number of years immersed in the study of Revelation, and it has been a fascinating study. The focus of my work was to study the best scholarship on Revelation, then draw from that scholarship to write a study guide that is directed to lay people and congregational use. That study guide has taken shape as this book. My hope is that this book will serve as a bridge between academic study and the ongoing life of the people of God.

I need also add that in the course of my studies, I have come to see Revelation as a tremendous gift and as a powerful proclamation of the Word of God. It is a Word that has spoken powerfully to Christians through the ages and it is a Word that still proclaims a vital message for us today. I hope this book helps you to hear this Word from God, and to sense the power and wonder of the God revealed in the Lamb who was slain.

Many thanks are due for making this book possible. A deep thank you must be said to Dr. Craig Koester of Luther Seminary, my advisor for my Doctor of Ministry work. I very much appreciate all the hours and insights Dr. Koester so freely shared. His insights and critiques and guidance have been invaluable. Thank you also to Dr. Matthew Skinner of Luther Seminary for his comments and critiques of this manuscript.

Thank you to the good people of Our Saviour's Lutheran Church in Tyler, Texas, and Grace Lutheran Church in Fairmont, Minnesota. They have allowed me to study Revelation with them and teach Revelation for them. In their questions and comments, I have gained insight into the book and a sense of how Revelation is a vital Word for the whole people of God.

Thank you to Dad and Mom, LaVerne and Lucille Braaten, for your support and help in making my Doctor of Ministry studies possible. You instilled in me a love for learning and teaching, and that love guided this project. Thank you to my children, Amber, Christopher, and Cassaundra. Your encouragement and support through these years of study has been so important to me. Your excitement keeps refreshing me.

And most of all, thank you to my wife Karen. In your love I've been empowered and uplifted for ministry, for writing, for life. Thanks for sharing my life, for keeping our home and family going, and for supporting me in all these projects that I keep finding.

May God guide us all by his Word into newness of life.

Introduction

A pastor served as chaplain in a nursing home. One of the residents of the home was a man who was mentally challenged. This man was a person of deep Christian faith. He was constantly going to worship, and loved to talk about the faith.

One afternoon the pastor and the man were talking about the Bible. The pastor asked the man what his favorite book of the Bible was. The man replied, "Revelation." The pastor was intrigued. He asked the man if he understood the book. The man said, "Sure." The pastor asked the man what the message of Revelation is. The man smiled and said, "Jesus wins in the end."[1]

Jesus wins. That's a good introduction to the book of Revelation. Also, it must be quickly added, we are invited to share in Jesus' victory.

Revelation is a powerful book. Its images and choruses and proclamations contain profound witness to the Lordship of Jesus Christ. More than any other book of the Bible, Revelation lifts up the victory and the hope of Jesus. Underlying the entire book is the conviction that Jesus has conquered, and the invitation is issued that we conquer with him. Revelation is a profound and fitting final book of the Bible.

Revelation is also a confusing book. There is no book in the Bible that has so exasperated Christians, nor any book that has been so misinterpreted. Many a devout Christian has read into Revelation, only to close the book in frustration. Many people have come up with wild and differing understandings of the book, which serve to further the confusion. Too often the message of Revelation seems beyond our grasp and we simply avoid it.

This study is written with the conviction that Revelation contains a message that can not only be understood, but which can powerfully direct our faith. As we examine and appreciate the rich symbolism of

---

[1] This story is told by Rev. Paul T. Hadland of Augustana Lutheran Church in Fergus Falls, MN.

Revelation, we find an incredible message. Even more, as we study Revelation, we encounter the Word of God. Through the pages of Revelation, the Holy Spirit speaks, and we are guided and shaped in lives of faith.

Five Background Questions

Before we begin our reading of Revelation, we need some background information. Let's look at five questions that will aid us in our journey.

1. *Who* wrote Revelation?
2. *Where* was it written, and where are the churches to which it was sent?
3. *When* was Revelation written?
4. *How* is the book to be understood?
5. *Why* should we read Revelation?

Who wrote Revelation?

The author of Revelation identifies himself as John. In 1:9 he writes, "I, John, your brother who share with you in Jesus the persecution and the kingdom and the patient endurance." John is obviously someone well known to the original recipients of Revelation, and requires no further introduction to them. Unfortunately, we know very little about him.

There is an old tradition in the church that says that the author of Revelation is also the author of the Gospel of John, and is John the son of Zebedee, one of the original disciples. This tradition dates back to the second century.[2] However, there are numerous reasons for questioning the accuracy of this tradition.

The first reason for questioning this tradition is that it is doubtful that the author of Revelation is John the son of Zebedee, one of the original disciples. If that were the case, the author of Revelation would have been a very old man by the time he wrote Revelation. He would have been in his eighties or nineties. Moreover, in the book itself, the author simply introduces himself as "brother" (1:9). He makes no claim to be an apostle, nor to have shared in Jesus' earthly ministry. (In fact, in 21:14, the author mentions the twelve apostles of Jesus, but makes no attempt to link himself to the apostles.) Given this, it appears that the author is not John the disciple.

---

[2] Adela Yarbro Collins, *Crisis and Catharsis: The Power of the Apocalypse* (Philadelphia: The Westminster Press, 1984), 25–26.

There is a second issue here, and that is that it is also quite doubtful that the book of Revelation and the Gospel of John have the same author. The two works differ enough in style, vocabulary, and theology that it seems unlikely that they were written by the same person.

We do best not to identify the author of Revelation with John the disciple, or with the author of the Fourth Gospel. But that leaves us with the question, who then is this John who wrote Revelation? We know little about him, only what we find in the book. John was obviously a person who knew the seven churches in Revelation well. We know that he had been banished by the Romans to the island of Patmos for preaching the Word of God (1:9). He was a person of deep faith, who considered his work a work of prophecy. Beyond this we know little about him.

Perhaps it is significant that we know little about John. John's intention in writing Revelation was not to point us to himself, but to point us to Jesus. He has succeeded in doing just that.

**Where was Revelation written,
and where are the churches to which it was sent?**

John tells us that he wrote Revelation on the island of Patmos (1:9). Patmos is a small island in the Aegean Sea, about forty miles off the coast of modern day Turkey. As was noted, John had been banished to Patmos by the Romans because of his preaching and teaching.

Revelation is addressed "to the seven churches that are in Asia" (1:4). Asia refers to the Roman province of Asia, which was the western part of Asia Minor, or modern day Turkey. Revelation is specifically addressed to seven congregations that are spread across the western half of Asia Minor.

This, however, raises a question. Why is Revelation addressed to only seven churches? We know from the New Testament and from church history that there were more than seven congregations in the Roman province of Asia. Why is Revelation addressed to only seven?

There are two possibilities here. One is that John simply chose to write to seven specific churches. Perhaps these were the congregations he knew best; perhaps he had other reasons for writing to these seven. A second possibility is to be found in the symbolism of Revelation. Seven was a number that implied completeness. (John will repeatedly use the number seven as a symbol of completeness throughout Revelation. There will be seven seals, seven trumpets, seven bowls, etc.) Given this, perhaps the seven churches that are mentioned are to represent the entire or the complete church. John's message, while directed specifically to seven congregations, would also be an open letter intended for the church as a whole.

We can't be sure which of these possibilities is correct. We are sure, however, of two things. First, John takes the specific context of the seven congregations very seriously. Revelation is addressed to seven specific congregations and, as we will see in chapters two and three of Revelation, John knows these seven congregations well. He is intimately aware of their lives, and of their strengths and weaknesses. The book is directed to a very specific context. Second, as part of the church of Christ, we can read John's words with attention to what they say to and about our own congregations.

When was Revelation written?

Revelation was most likely written at the end of the first century. The book itself does not give a date of composition. There are however two reasons for dating the book toward the end of the first century. First, and most importantly, there was an early Christian leader named Irenaeus who lived in the later second century, who wrote a major work around 180 A.D. entitled *Against Heresies.* In this work Irenaeus said that Revelation was written at the end of the reign of the Roman Emperor Domitian, who ruled from 81 to 96 A.D. That would date the book of Revelation around 95 or 96 A.D.

A second reason for dating Revelation to the end of the first century is that Revelation often uses the name "Babylon" for Rome. (For example, see chapter 17 of Revelation, especially verses 5 and 9. The city is referred to as "Babylon," but is also identified as the city on seven hills, a definite reference to Rome.) This way of referring to Rome as Babylon developed in Judaism after 70 A.D., when the Romans destroyed Jerusalem and the Jewish temple. John's use of this terminology would point to a date in the later first century.

Given all this, a late first century date is quite probable. Of course we can't be certain. But following Irenaeus, 95 or 96 A.D. seems likely.

How is Revelation to be understood?

Revelation is a challenging book. It contains strange pictures and imageries. Its thoughts and patterns seem foreign to us. We wonder how we are to approach the book. As we seek to understand Revelation, it is helpful to keep four categories in mind. Revelation is a letter, a prophecy, an apocalypse, and a spiral of visions.[3] Each of these categories is helpful in understanding the book.

A Letter

Revelation is a letter, written by a man named John to a number of churches in the Roman province of Asia. It contains standard formats of Christian letters from the first century—greetings, blessings, listing of sender and recipients. Moreover, Revelation has many similarities in form to the letters of Paul. Just like the letters of Paul, Revelation is a letter that John expected to be read aloud in the worship of the receiving congregations.

It is important to keep this in mind, for this reminds us that Revelation was not originally addressed to us. John did not address his message to twenty-first-century Christians. Revelation was originally intended for first-century Christians in Asia Minor. Given that, we do well in our studies of Revelation to ask first what Revelation said to its original audience. After that we can ask what it says to us. Of course Revelation still speaks powerfully and vitally to our modern day. But we do well to begin our studies by remembering that Revelation was originally directed to someone else.

A Prophecy

John identifies the book of Revelation as being a prophecy (1:3). Since John considered his work to be words of prophecy, we do well to ask what that means. Please note, we need to be very careful here, because John has a different understanding of prophecy than we do. We think of prophecy in terms of foretelling the future. We see prophecy as "history written in advance," or as being about predictions of future events, but John has a different understanding.

For John there are two elements in prophecy. First, prophecy is an inspired message, received directly from God.[4] John received his message in a divinely given vision (1:2, 1:10), and he is careful to note that the message of Revelation is God's message.

[3] Craig R. Koester, *Revelation and the End of All Things* (William B. Eerdmans Publishing Company, 2001), 38–40, 42.

[4] M. Eugene Boring, *Revelation,* Interpretation, A Bible Commentary for Teaching and Preaching, ed. James Mays and Paul Achtemeier (Louisville: John Knox Press, 1989), 25.

Second, prophecy for John involves true testimony to Jesus. (Note, in 19:10b, John writes, "Worship God! For the testimony of Jesus is the spirit of prophecy.") The function of prophecy is to direct people to the one Lord Jesus Christ, and to call people to live in faithful obedience to this Lord. Prophecy is about directing people in the life of faith.

We need to be very careful here, for John's view of prophecy is different from ours. For John true prophecy is not so much about laying out a road map to the future, as it is about calling people to live for Jesus in both the present and the future. The focus of prophecy is in faithful teaching and exhortation.

Two examples from Revelation are helpful here. In 2:20 and following, John writes about a false prophet whom he calls "Jezebel." The reason that John labels this woman a false prophet is not because she has made inaccurate predictions about the future. In fact, there is no reference to any predictions. Rather "Jezebel" is teaching people to "practice fornication and to eat food sacrificed to idols" (2:20).[5] In her teaching she is not bearing true testimony to Jesus, and therefore she is a false prophet.

A second example is found in Revelation 11:3. In this passage there are two witnesses who are said to prophesy, but their message is not about the future. It is about repentance, as indicated by their being dressed in sackcloth. Their prophetic message is one that calls people to Jesus. That again is what prophecy is for John. It is a divinely given message that calls people to an active and true faith.

Now, the prophetic message certainly has implications for the future. John foresees the destruction of the Roman Empire, and he looks forward to the new heaven and the new earth. But prophecy also involves the present, as John calls the people of the seven churches to faithful living. Prophecy for John involves directing all of life to Jesus.

It is important that we understand John's view of prophecy, for this has implications for how we read Revelation. If we follow John's guidance, we will find in Revelation not so much a road map to the future, but a call for obedience and faithfulness. We do well to carefully let John guide us here.

An Apocalypse

Revelation is a type of literature that is called "apocalyptic literature." This type of literature developed in the ancient world and is often quite difficult for modern readers. "Apocalypse" is a Greek word that means

---

[5] Koester, 45–46.

"revelation" or "unveiling." (The word "apocalypse" is actually the first word in the original Greek text of the book of Revelation.) Eventually the word "apocalypse" came to be used to refer to this whole type of literature that developed from roughly 200 B.C. to 200 A.D. Revelation is one of the great examples of apocalyptic literature. Other examples can be found in both Jewish and Christian circles, and include works such as: Second Esdras, Sibylline Oracles, Second Baruch, and the second half of the Old Testament book of Daniel.

Apocalyptic literature was a picturesque, symbolic type of writing. It involved rich imagery and cosmic battles. Apocalyptic literature often included angels, supernatural beings, plagues and trials, and battles between God and Satan. Often it focused on the end of the world. Apocalyptic literature was expressive, pronounced, and made use of rich and often bizarre images (seven-headed dragons, cosmic events, etc.). It was concerned with justice, that God and God's people be vindicated in a sinful world. It often contained words of warning for nonbelievers, and words of encouragement for believers. One of the functions of apocalyptic literature was to provide hope for people in difficult situations.

The following is an example of a non-Biblical piece of apocalyptic literature. It is found in a work entitled Second Esdras, specifically chapter 5, verses 1-7.

> Now concerning the signs: behold, the days are coming, when those who dwell on earth shall be seized with great terror, and the way of truth shall be hidden, and the land shall be barren of faith. [2]And unrighteousness shall be increased beyond what you yourself see, and beyond what you heard of formerly. [3]And the land which you now see ruling shall be waste and untrodden, and men shall see it desolate. [4]But if the Most High grants that you live, you shall see it thrown into confusion after the third period; and the sun shall suddenly shine forth at night, and the moon during the day. [5]Blood shall drip from wood, and the stone shall utter its voice; the peoples shall be troubled, and the stars shall fall. [6]And one shall reign whom those who dwell on earth do not expect, and the birds shall fly away together; [7]and the sea of Sodom shall cast up fish; and one whom the many do not know shall make his voice heard by night, and all shall hear his voice.[6]

Note the vivid imagery and threats of judgment. Sin and evil will be dealt with. Implicit in the judgment is a promise of deliverance for

[6] Bruce Metzger, ed., *The Oxford Annotated Apocrypha Revised Standard Version* (New York: Oxford University Press, Inc., 1977), 31.

the righteous. This type of imagery and this message are common in apocalyptic literature; in fact, we will find similar imagery and messages in the book of Revelation.

As modern readers we are not familiar with apocalyptic literature. We tend to see Revelation as a unique piece of literature. We wonder how John came up with such strange and bizarre images. It is helpful to recognize that Revelation is not the only piece of literature like this. It is rather an example (and a very good example!) of a type of literature that existed in Jewish and Christian circles of the time. John's images, rather than being simply bizarre, fit in well with this type of literature. John is using a specific style of writing to share his vision and to proclaim the Word of God.

We also need to remember that John's first readers would have been familiar with this type of writing, and would have known how to grasp the images and message of Revelation. In fact, John expected that his first audience would hear and understand his work as it was read in worship (1:3).

The challenge we modern readers have is that this style of writing is strange to us. It strikes us as confusing and even incomprehensible. However, modern readers can come to understand the messages and the images of Revelation. We will need to work at it, but as we do, we will find that Revelation proclaims a vital and powerful Word!

A Spiral of Visions

Another helpful insight in understanding Revelation is to recognize that Revelation is a cyclic book, a book that contains cycles of visions, repetitions, and deepening developments of reoccurring themes. Revelation is written as a spiral, with ideas and themes developed, then redeveloped and intensified as the book moves onward.

Too often we try to read Revelation in a straight-moving, chronological manner. We assume that the book moves from point A to point B to point C. But the problem is, the book isn't written that way, and reading it in such a manner only creates confusion or misunderstanding.

Part of John's artistry is that he repeats and redevelops ideas in a cyclic manner. John will develop point A and point B. But then rather than moving on to point C, he will return to point A and redevelop and deepen that idea. Revelation is an artistic work, in which John uses a spiral of visions to proclaim the glory and power of God.

Three examples are helpful in seeing this. First, at the end of chapter 6, when the sixth seal is opened, the universe comes to an end. The sun becomes black, the stars fall to the earth, and the sky vanishes (6:12-14). The cosmos is finished. That would seem to indicate the end of the book. And yet it does not. The opening of the next seal, rather than announcing the end, instead opens up a whole new series of events, the seven trumpets.

Second, when the seventh trumpet is blown in chapter 11, we again seem to come to the end. Verse 11:19 tells us that God's temple in heaven is opened, and the ark of the covenant is seen within the temple. In Jewish thought, this is an announcement of the end of history, and the coming of the fullness of God's kingdom. But again the book does not end here. Rather, a new series of visions begins.

Third, Babylon (or Rome) is said to be destroyed in a variety of ways. It is destroyed by an earthquake (16:19), by its former allies (17:16), and by pestilence, mourning, famine, and fire (18:8). To read this in a straightforward, chronological manner raises all sorts of problems. (For example, how many times is Rome to be destroyed?) We do better to read this as a repetitious, intensifying message of John's conviction that Rome will be judged, and that Christians must avoid compromise with Roman ways.

Revelation is not written in a chronological manner. Rather, like a powerful hymn, the messages are repeated in ongoing verses and refrains. John repeats, redevelops, and expands his themes in an ever-intensifying spiral of visions. The result is a powerful proclaiming of the Word and wonder of God.

Why should we read Revelation?

Given all the challenges in reading Revelation, the final question to ask is why should we read it? Three answers stand out.

First, we read Revelation because it is part of the Bible. The church has determined that Revelation is part of its authoritative writings, the Holy Scripture. As such, Revelation speaks the Word of God in a normative and definitive way. We as Christians need to know this Word. To avoid Revelation (or other parts of the Bible for that matter) is to shortchange the life of faith.

Second, Revelation has greatly informed the hymns and worship life of the church. An intriguing fact about Revelation is that while many Christians avoid reading the book, they nonetheless sing the book. Many of the great hymns of the church and other portions of worship come from the book of Revelation.

Here is a partial listing of some hymns that draw from the book of Revelation:

"Holy, Holy, Holy"
"All Hail the Power of Jesus' Name"
"Crown Him with Many Crowns"
"For All the Saints"
"Battle Hymn of the Republic"
"Shall We Gather at the River"
"Jerusalem, My Happy Home"
"Hallelujah Chorus" of Handel's *Messiah*

Moreover, the choruses and announcements of Revelation have been and continue to be used in the worship life of the church. For example, the hymn of praise "Worthy is Christ" in the *Lutheran Book of Worship* is a composition based on the hymns of Revelation.[7] Note the words, and as we read into Revelation, listen for these themes:

Worthy is Christ, the Lamb who was slain,
Whose blood set us free to be people of God.
Power and riches and wisdom and strength,
and honor and blessing and glory are His.
This is the feast of victory for our God. Alleluia.
Sing with all the people of God and join in the hymn of all creation:
Blessing and honor and glory and might be to God and the Lamb
    forever. Amen.
This is the feast of victory for our God,
    for the Lamb who was slain has begun His reign. Alleluia. Alleluia.[8]

Often Christians don't study the book of Revelation, but they sing the book in their hymns. The words of Revelation continue to enrich and inform the church's worship life. We do well to read and study this rich resource.

Third, Revelation speaks a Word of God that is vital for Christians today. Many of the issues in Revelation are issues that Christians continue to wrestle with in our day: issues of complacency in faith, of accommodation to culture, of persecution for the faith, of hope in a challenging world. In Revelation we encounter a message that shapes and informs the life of faith in the twenty-first century.

---

[7] Philip H. Pfatteicher and Carlos R. Messerli, *Manual on the Liturgy: Lutheran Book of Worship* (Minneapolis: Augsburg Publishing House, 1979), 213.

[8] *Lutheran Book of Worship* (Minneapolis: Augsburg Publishing House, 1978), 81.

We have noted that Revelation was not originally addressed to twenty-first century Christians. That is true, and we need to keep that in mind as we study the book. But the wonder of Revelation is that it nonetheless continues to speak to new generations of Christians, including ours. Revelation has spoken to Christians for nearly two thousand years. Our generation too needs to hear this Word from our God.

Section I
A Vision of Christ
Chapter 1

This first section is an introduction to the book of Revelation. It identifies Revelation as a letter from John to seven congregations in ancient Asia Minor. Note how this opening section is dominated by a vision of Jesus. John begins by focusing us on Jesus Christ.

Chapter 1

> **1:1-3**
>
> The revelation of Jesus Christ, which God gave him to show his servants what must soon take place; he made it known by sending his angel to his servant John, [2]who testified to the word of God and to the testimony of Jesus Christ, even to all that he saw.
>
> [3]Blessed is the one who reads aloud the words of the prophecy, and blessed are those who hear and who keep what is written in it; for the time is near.

John begins the book by pointing to Jesus. This book will be "the revelation of Jesus Christ" given by God. John is clear from line one. This book is a message from God, and Jesus is the means by which God shares this message. We as modern readers need to read the book with this in mind. This is a message from God and is to be treated and understood as such.

It is worth noting that our modern Bibles usually entitle the book "The Revelation to John." This title is a later addition, and a bit of a misnomer, for it focuses on the author. John has no intention of focusing on himself. He rather directs us to God, the God revealed in Jesus Christ.

John goes on to explain more about the origins of this revelation. This message came by a chain. It is rooted in God, and then proceeded from God to Jesus to an angel to John. (This type of chain is common in apocalyptic literature. It served to ensure the transcendence of God.) Make no mistake, John insists. John is writing the manuscript, but the author is the Almighty.

The introduction then proceeds with a blessing, both to the one who reads the book and to those who hear and keep the words of the book. In the ancient world, most reading was out loud. John expects this book to be read out loud during worship. Those who read and hear the book are blessed.[1]

John refers to his words as "prophecy." It is important to note again that for John, prophecy was not a road map to the future. Prophecy was

---

[1] This blessing is the first of seven blessings in the book. As was previously pointed out, John often uses the number seven. In the ancient world, seven was a number that symbolized completeness, fullness. The seven blessings point to the fullness of blessing that is given in Jesus Christ.

teaching and exhortation, given by God, that directed people to Jesus. That is why John tells people to "keep" what is written. We keep prophecy by obeying it in lives faithful to Jesus.

John goes on to add, "the time is near." This will be a reoccurring announcement in the book. John will tell us numerous times that "Jesus is coming soon" and that "the time is near." As we move through the book, we will need to discuss what John means by this. For now we will simply note that this language adds a real urgency to the message. This prophecy must be read and heard and lived immediately!

1:4-8

[4]John to the seven churches that are in Asia: Grace to you and peace from him who is and who was and who is to come, and from the seven spirits who are before his throne, [5]and from Jesus Christ, the faithful witness, the firstborn of the dead, and the ruler of the kings of the earth.

To him who loves us and freed us from our sins by his blood, [6]and made us to be a kingdom, priests serving his God and Father, to him be glory and dominion forever and ever. Amen.

[7]Look! He is coming with the clouds; every eye will see him, even those who pierced him; and on his account all the tribes of the earth will wail. So it is to be. Amen.

[8]"I am the Alpha and the Omega," says the Lord God, who is and who was and who is to come, the Almighty.

This new section reveals that the book is actually a letter. It is a letter from John to seven churches in Asia. (Asia refers to the Roman province of Asia, which is roughly the western half of modern day Turkey.) John, much like St. Paul in preceding years, writes a letter to congregations. In verse 4 and after, John follows some of the format of Paul. (For example, compare 1:4 with 1 Corinthians 1:1-3.) This is a particular letter addressed to seven specific congregations.

John begins with "grace to you and peace." This was a standard Christian greeting, and one that is often still used in worship today. John writes that grace and peace come from God, who is described as him "who is and who was and who is to come." This designation echoes the Old Testament name of God as found in Exodus 3:14 ("I am who I am"). God is the everlasting one, the one who has always been and who always will be. But John wants to tell us even more than that, and writes that God "is to come." The future of God will be defined by his coming on behalf of this world.

John has more to tell us about God. God's throne is surrounded by seven spirits. This is a reference to Jewish thought, where seven spiritual beings stand before the throne of God. Perhaps it is also the case that this "seven" functions symbolically and is an indication of completeness and fullness. If that is the case, then what we have here is a reference to the one, complete, Holy Spirit of God.

Grace and peace are also said to come from Jesus Christ. Jesus is intimately linked with God, both here and throughout the book of Revelation. Revelation in fact has one of the most exalted views of Jesus in the New Testament. Jesus is further described as "the faithful witness, the firstborn of the dead, and the ruler of the kings of the earth." All of these images will become important in the book. "The ruler of the kings of the earth" is a politically loaded statement. To Roman minds, the ruler of the kings was the Roman emperor. John challenges that and says that highest authority belongs to Jesus.

Verses 4 and 5 raise a question for modern readers. Do we have in these lines a Trinitarian statement? In other words, does this language of God and the seven spirits and Jesus Christ point us to the one God who is Father, Spirit, and Son? That is a difficult question to answer, as we can't be sure what was in the mind of John. On the one hand, we need to be careful about reading later ideas into the text. The doctrine of the Trinity wasn't fully developed until a few hundred years after John wrote Revelation. But on the other hand, John seems to be moving in that direction. John points us to a fuller proclamation of the mystery of God.

John continues by telling us more about Jesus. Jesus is the one who "loves us and freed us and made us to be a kingdom of priests serving God." Note the incredible things that Jesus has done for his people. Moreover, Jesus is the one "to whom be glory and dominion forever." Once again we have an incredibly powerful view of Jesus.

John then shifts focus and tells us that Jesus will come again. But this coming is more threat than comfort, as "all the tribes of the earth will wail." This is a word of warning for those who ignore Jesus. "The tribes" are those who have not taken Jesus seriously, and John tells us that they will be judged (i.e. "will wail") at Jesus' coming. John has set up a stark contrast here. In the previous paragraph John has written about the love and freedom and kingdom that Jesus' followers share. Now in this section, John adds that those who have not taken Jesus seriously will wail at his coming. John's not-so-subtle question of us is, where will we be? Will we be part of the community that shares in the glory of Jesus, or part of the tribes that wail at his coming?

Note also how John has constructed this last paragraph. Verse 7 is a paraphrase of Old Testament verses Daniel 7:13 and Zechariah 12:10 and 12. It is not an exact quotation, but a paraphrase of these verses. A point to watch in Revelation is that John will continually allude to the Old Testament. He will never quote the Old Testament directly. But he will allude to it, and paraphrase it, hundreds of times. The Old Testament is one of the key sources from which John draws his imagery.

This section concludes with another key phrase for God. God is the "Alpha and the Omega," which are the first and last letters of the Greek alphabet. He is the "a" and the "z," the first and the last. As John has already stated, God is the one "who is and who was and who is to come."

1:9-11

⁹I, John, your brother who share with you in Jesus the persecution and the kingdom and the patient endurance, was on the island called Patmos because of the word of God and the testimony of Jesus. ¹⁰I was in the spirit on the Lord's day, and I heard behind me a loud voice like a trumpet ¹¹saying, "Write in a book what you see and send it to the seven churches, to Ephesus, to Smyrna, to Pergamum, to Thyatira, to Sardis, to Philadelphia, and to Laodicea."

John once again introduces himself, this time as a "brother" who shares with the people the life of faith. John makes no claim to being one of the original twelve apostles. He is obviously someone well known to the recipients, as he feels no need for further introduction. He emphasizes that he shares with the Christians "the persecution, the kingdom, and the patient endurance." As we will see, these items are central to John's understanding of the Christian life.

John writes that he was on the island called Patmos, which is an island about forty miles off the coast of modern day Turkey. Most likely he was banished there by the Romans for his preaching and teaching activities. John further explains that he was "in the spirit on the Lord's day" when he saw and heard a message. We're not sure exactly what John means by this. Was he in prayer, in worship, in a vision, or in some other spiritual experience? Whatever the exact experience, we need to take John at his word here. John received a revelation as a gift from God, and he shares it in this book.

Two points are worth noting here. First, spiritual experiences were well accepted in New Testament times. For example, Peter has a vision in Acts 10:10 and Paul records that he was caught up into the third heaven in 2 Corinthians 12:2-3. John seems to have had some sort of similar experience. Second, John does not focus on his own experience, but on the message that God gave him. For John what is vital is not what happened to him, but the message that God shared.

John continues by recording that he heard a voice. We learn later that this is the voice of Jesus. John is instructed to write what he sees in a book, and send it to the seven churches, which are listed here for the first time.

1:12-20

[12]Then I turned to see whose voice it was that spoke to me, and on turning I saw seven golden lampstands, [13]and in the midst of the lampstands I saw one like the Son of Man, clothed with a long robe and with a golden sash across his chest. [14]His head and his hair were white as white wool, white as snow; his eyes were like a flame of fire, [15]his feet were like burnished bronze, refined as in a furnace, and his voice was like the sound of many waters. [16]In his right hand he held seven stars, and from his mouth came a sharp, two-edged sword, and his face was like the sun shining with full force.

[17]When I saw him, I fell at his feet as though dead. But he placed his right hand on me, saying, "Do not be afraid; I am the first and the last, [18]and the living one. I was dead, and see, I am alive forever and ever; and I have the keys of Death and of Hades. [19]Now write what you have seen, what is and what is to take place after this. [20]As for the mystery of the seven stars that you saw in my right hand, and the seven golden lampstands: the seven stars are the angels of the seven churches, and the seven lampstands are the seven churches.

John turns to see who has spoken to him. As he turns he sees seven golden lampstands, and someone standing in the midst of the lampstands. We learn in verse 20 that the seven lampstands symbolize the seven churches, and we learn from the rich imagery that the person is Jesus. Jesus stands in the midst of his churches. We are reminded that Jesus is not an absentee Lord. He is present in the very midst of his people.

Jesus is then described in rich imagery, rooted in the Old Testament. "One like a Son of Man" draws on Daniel 7:13. The robe and sash are clothes of the High Priest in Exodus 28:4. The white hair is a mark of the Ancient of Days (God) in Daniel 7:9. Eyes like a flame of fire, feet like burnished bronze, and the voice of many waters draw from Daniel 10:5-6.

The two-edged sword represents the Word of God as in Isaiah 49:2. Further, Jesus shines "like the sun shining with full force." What we have here is an image of the wonder and majesty of the Savior. We ought to stand back and simply be in awe!

Note the language that John uses. He uses the words "like" and "as." The challenge that John has is, how does one describe Jesus in his full glory? There is simply no adequate language for doing that. So John uses the langue of symbolism and simile to paint a picture of the glory of Jesus. We can analyze this picture and take it apart and understand what the various symbols point out. But we also need to step back and simply see and experience the images. What we have here is a powerful picture of the living Christ.

In verse 17 John falls at Jesus' feet, as though dead. This is an appropriate response when one finds oneself face to face with the living Lord! But Jesus tells John not to be afraid. Jesus says that he is the "first and the last" (note the echo of Alpha and Omega from verse 8) and the one who died and rose again. In addition he is the one who has "the keys of Death and of Hades," the one who sets people free from death. Jesus then instructs John to write the vision.

The book of Revelation begins with a vision of Jesus, the glorified Jesus, the Jesus who is present now. Jesus in Revelation (and in the entire New Testament for that matter!) is the one in whom God accomplishes his purposes of redemption and salvation. One of the focuses of this book is to help people (including us!) encounter Jesus Christ.

Chapter 1 ends by pointing out that the seven lampstands are the seven churches, and the seven stars are the angels of the seven churches. John will speak of angels quite a bit, and in the next chapter he will address his remarks to the angels of the seven churches. Apocalyptic literature as a whole often uses the imagery of angels. Perhaps Revelation serves to remind modern Christians that there is more in this universe than our scientific minds see!

John's Use of Symbols

This is a good place to look at how John uses symbols, and to point out that John uses symbols to speak of and to point to deeper realities. We need to be careful in Revelation not to take the symbols literally. We rather need to ask, what is John saying when he uses symbols? Two examples are helpful. First, when John says that Jesus has white hair, he is really not concerned about Jesus' hair color. He rather is telling us that

Jesus is the Ancient of Days (Dan 7:9), and thereby shares in the wonder of God. Second, when John writes that "from his mouth came a sharp, two-edged sword," we ought not to think of a dagger that hangs from Jesus' teeth. (If that image is literally true, it becomes impossible and grotesque.) It is rather symbolism drawn from Isaiah 49 that proclaims that Jesus is the one who truly speaks the Word of God. When John uses symbols, we need to ask what the symbols say.

John uses symbols to speak of and point to deeper realities. This needs to be recognized now, and remembered as we proceed with the book. Too often when people go further on in Revelation and come to things like Armageddon and 666 and the thousand-year reign, they forget that these too are symbols, and not to be taken literally. We do well to continually ask how John uses his symbols, and let that show us how to understand the message.

Section II
Messages to the Seven Churches

Chapters 2–3

This section consists of seven messages to seven specific congregations. John, following the directive of Jesus, turns his attention to the seven churches. Jesus has a specific message for each of the congregations, a message in which the unique situation of each congregation is examined and evaluated. John obviously knows these congregations well. He commends them for their faithfulness; he chastises them for their failings. He urges them onward in faith.

A good question to ask of these messages is, do any of these congregations sound like the one to which we belong? Which congregation or congregations are we most like? Or to push the question even further, what would John have to say to us in our modern congregations?

Chapter 2

In chapters 2 and 3, John writes a specific message to each of the seven churches. The messages all follow the same basic pattern,[1] which can be summarized as follows:

- Address to the angel/congregation (including identification of Christ)
- Words of rebuke, commendation, and encouragement
- Call to listen and promise to the conquerors

Three additional things need to be pointed out about these messages. First, these messages are addressed to the "angel of the church." John seems to assume that each congregation has a heavenly representative. However, the message is clearly meant for the entire congregation.

Second, at the end of each of the seven messages, John refers to the faithful as "conquerors." This is an important concept in Revelation, and we will see it throughout the book. To conquer is a military metaphor, which reminds the first readers, and modern-day readers, that it is a struggle to be faithful. Moreover, John has a unique definition of how we conquer. As we will see as we read into the book, we conquer by being faithful to Christ, even to the point of dying for the faith.

Third, these messages are from Jesus and are given through John. John is the one writing the messages, but John insists that the messages are ultimately from Jesus.

2:1-7

"To the angel of the church in Ephesus write: These are the words of him who holds the seven stars in his right hand, who walks among the seven golden lampstands:

[2]"I know your works, your toil and your patient endurance. I know that you cannot tolerate evildoers; you have tested those who claim to be apostles but are not, and have found them to be false. [3]I also know that you are enduring patiently and bearing up for the sake of my name, and that you have not grown weary. [4]But I have this against you, that you have abandoned the love you had at first. [5]Remember then from what you have

---

[1] Craig Koester, *Revelation and the End of All Things* (Grand Rapids, MI: William Eerdmans Publishing Company, 2001), 56.

> fallen; repent, and do the works you did at first. If not, I will come to you and remove your lampstand from its place, unless you repent. [6]Yet this is to your credit: you hate the works of the Nicolaitans, which I also hate. [7]Let anyone who has an ear listen to what the Spirit is saying to the churches. To everyone who conquers, I will give permission to eat from the tree of life that is in the paradise of God.

Ephesus was the principal city of Asia Minor, with a population of about 250,000. It was located on the coast of the Aegean Sea, and was wealthy and cosmopolitan. Ephesus had a huge temple to the goddess Artemis, which was considered one of the wonders of the ancient world. There were also temples to the goddess Roma, to Julius Caesar, and by the end of the first century, to the emperor Domitian. There had been a Christian congregation in Ephesus since the mid-first century. According to Acts 20:31, Paul spent three years at Ephesus.

John begins this message by drawing from the image of Christ in chapter 1. These are the words of him who holds the seven stars and who walks among the seven golden lampstands. The point is stressed—this message is rooted and given in Jesus.

The church in Ephesus is commended for its patient endurance. It has toiled hard and diligently. Likewise, the congregation has been doctrinally pure, and has resisted the claims of false teachers and apostles. ("Apostle" literally means "one who is sent out." It refers to more than the original twelve disciples. The term refers to numerous teachers and missionaries, some of whom were teaching false doctrine.) But this purity of doctrine has come at a price. In their efforts to be doctrinally correct, the people have lost sight of love. The congregation is rebuked for abandoning the love they had at first.

Ephesus is instructed to repent, and find anew the love they once shared. If they do not, Christ threatens to come and remove their lampstand (i.e., they will cease to be Christ's church). The congregation is then commended once more, this time for opposing the Nicolaitans, a group that John also opposes. (We will talk about the Nicolaitans when we talk of Pergamum.) The message ends with an exhortation and a promise. The exhortation is to listen to these words, for they are words of the Spirit. The promise is that everyone who conquers will be allowed to eat from the tree of life in the paradise of God. As was previously mentioned, "to conquer" is to be faithful to Jesus, even unto death. "To eat of the tree of life" draws on Old Testament imagery and is the promise of eternal life in the grace of God. Those who are faithful are promised eternal life in God's paradise.

The message to Ephesus raises an issue that is important for the church throughout the ages. Love must not be sacrificed for doctrinal correctness. Ancient congregations and modern congregations all too easily get caught up in theological disputes, and in the process lose sight of compassion. The church must strive to be both correct in doctrine and diligent in love.

2:8-11

[8]"And to the angel of the church in Smyrna write: These are the words of the first and the last, who was dead and came to life:

[9]"I know your affliction and your poverty, even though you are rich. I know the slander on the part of those who say that they are Jews and are not, but are a synagogue of Satan. [10]Do not fear what you are about to suffer. Beware, the devil is about to throw some of you into prison so that you may be tested, and for ten days you will have affliction. Be faithful until death, and I will give you the crown of life. [11]Let anyone who has an ear listen to what the Spirit is saying to the churches. Whoever conquers will not be harmed by the second death.

Smyrna, like Ephesus, was a large and prosperous commercial center. It too was located on the coast of the Aegean Sea, on the site of what is now the Turkish city of Izmir. Ancient Smyrna was well known for its loyalty to Rome and for its ritual worship of the Roman emperor.[2] It was a cultural center and affluent.

John begins this message by again drawing from the image of Christ in chapter 1. "These are the words of the first and the last, who was dead and came to life." Again the point is that this message is rooted in Christ; in fact these are the words of Jesus! John next makes reference to the poverty of this Christian community. In contrast to the wealth of Smyrna as a whole, the Christian community is poor. John writes of their "affliction and poverty." Note how John has only words of commendation for this poor congregation. Though they are economically poor, they are in reality rich, meaning rich in faith.

John refers to the slander from Jews who are of the "synagogue of Satan." This reflects a growing struggle and separation between Jews

---

[2] Bruce Metzger, *Breaking the Code: Understanding the Book of Revelation* (Nashville: Abingdon Press, 1993), 33.

and Christians. At first Christians were seen as a group within Judaism, which allowed Christians the legal protections the Romans gave to the Jews. (The Romans were generally tolerant of Judaism because it was a long established religion.) By the time of the writing of Revelation, the separation between Jews and Christians was becoming more apparent. That left the Christians without the legal protection that Jews had, and subject to persecution.

Historically, we know of no widespread persecutions at this time. But Christians who were denounced as Christians could be taken before the civil authorities and asked to either reject their faith or face punishment. Most likely the "slander" of the Jews was to denounce the Christians to the Roman authorities. John also foresees that more persecutions will come. We know from history that John was correct. In 156 A.D., about sixty years after the writing of Revelation, the bishop of Smyrna, a man named Polycarp, was executed by the Romans for the faith.

John warns that some Christians would be thrown into prison, and they would be afflicted "for ten days." Rather than take the ten days as a literal number, we do well to hear it as simply a period of time. The Christians are warned that they will suffer for their faith. John further urges the Christians to be faithful even until death, and they will be rewarded with the crown of life. The crown is a symbol of victory, the promise of eternal life. John proclaims a message of hope to the Christians in Smyrna as they face suffering and persecution.

John ends this message by promising that those who conquer "will not be harmed by the second death." This is a phrase that is unique in the New Testament to Revelation. This idea will be more fully developed in chapter 20, especially 20:11-15. For now we will simply note that the first death is what happens when we physically die. The second death is what happens at the Final Judgment to those who have refused to follow Christ.

2:12-17

[12]"And to the angel of the church in Pergamum write: These are the words of him who has the sharp two-edged sword:

[13]"I know where you are living, where Satan's throne is. Yet you are holding fast to my name, and you did not deny your faith in me even in the days of Antipas my witness, my faithful one, who was killed among you, where Satan lives. [14]But I have a few things against you: you have some there who hold to the teachings of Balaam, who taught Balak to put a stumbling block before the people of Israel, so that they would eat food

> sacrificed to idols and practice fornication. ¹⁵So you also have some who hold to the teachings of the Nicolaitans. ¹⁶Repent then. If not, I will come to you soon and make war against them with the sword of my mouth. ¹⁷Let anyone who has an ear listen to what the Spirit is saying to the churches. To everyone who conquers I will give some of the hidden manna, and I will give a white stone, and on the white stone is written a new name that no one knows except the one who receives it.

Pergamum was the seat of the Roman government in the province of Asia. It was a cultural center, and the home of a large and famous library. (Our English word "parchment" is derived from the word "Pergamum."[3]) In the midst of Pergamum stood a huge hill, on top of which were the Roman offices and buildings. In addition, on the top of the hill was a huge altar to Zeus and a temple for the emperor Augustus. The city as a whole had many temples and places of worship, including a sanctuary for Asclepius, the god of healing.

John begins the message to Pergamum by referring to Jesus as "the one who has the sharp two-edged sword." Once again the message is rooted in the vision of Christ from chapter 1. John is perhaps also making a point with his use of this imagery.[4] The Roman government of Asia was centered in Pergamum. The symbol of Roman power was the sword. Perhaps John chooses the image of a two-edged sword here to remind people that the real power is in the Word of God. It is Jesus Christ, and not the Roman officials, who finally wields power!

John in verse 13 writes that the people in Pergamum are living "where Satan's throne is." This might be a reference to one of the pagan temples, or to Roman power that is centralized there. It is perhaps a general term for the overall threat to Christians in Pergamum.[5] Another intriguing possibility is that most of the Roman government buildings and many of the pagan temples were located on the top of the large hill inside Pergamum. John is perhaps referring to those pagan influences which are "enthroned" on that hill as being the throne of Satan.

John then commends the congregation. The Christians have been faithful, even in the face of these challenges. In fact a Christian named Antipas has been put to death in Pergamum, and the congregation has

[3] Ibid., 24.
[4] G.B. Caird, *A Commentary on the Revelation of Saint John the Divine* (New York: Harper & Row, 1966), 37.
[5] Koester, 59.

held firm. In the face of outside persecution, the congregation has been faithful.

But there is a problem and it is from internal false teachings. John points out that some in the congregation "hold to the teachings of Balaam." Balaam is not the real name of John's opponent. Balaam was originally an Old Testament character who in Numbers 31:16 is said to have taught the people of Israel to live unfaithfully. John nicknames his opponent in Pergamum Balaam as a way of pointing out that this opponent is teaching falsely.

There are two issues in the teaching of Balaam. First is the issue of eating meat that has been sacrificed to idols. By way of background, much of the meat in ancient cites was slaughtered in pagan temples. Animals were brought to the temple and killed. Some of the meat was offered in pagan sacrifice; the rest was then sold in the markets. Christians struggled with whether or not they could eat such meat. This problem became compounded when Christians tried to participate in civic functions and trade guilds. Often civic functions would include meals that served meat that had been sacrificed to idols. If the Christians did not participate in the activities and the meals, they would become more and more outsiders of the society.

The second issue is that Balaam allowed people to "practice fornication." This could refer to sexual abuses, but most likely refers to the problem of emperor worship. In the Old Testament, the term "fornication" often was used not for sexual sins but for the sin of worshiping other gods. That seems to be the issue here. In the first century A.D., there was the growing practice of emperor worship. Temples were erected to the emperor; emperors were referred to as "son of god" or "lord and god." (Generally emperors were referred to as "lord and god" only after their deaths, although in the cases of Nero and Domitian the practice was used during their reign.) This emperor worship was particularly taking root in the eastern parts of the empire, which included the province of Asia.

It needs to be stated that many of the Romans didn't take this practice too seriously. A few Roman emperors encouraged the practice, others didn't. For many Romans, speaking of emperors as "lord and god" was not so much a religious confession as a sign of obedience to the state. However, Christians struggled with the practice.

These two issues of meat sacrificed to idols and emperor worship raised a basic question for the Christians, the question of accommodation. When does faith allow Christians to participate in society, and when does faith dictate that Christians must refuse to participate in society?

Balaam was teaching that Christians could accommodate themselves to these Roman practices. We can imagine some of his arguments. In regards to meat offered to idols, Balaam could argue that we know that idols have no real existence, so we are free to eat the meat. (In fact Balaam could appeal to Paul in 1 Corinthians 8.) Moreover, Balaam could argue that Christians should be involved in the activities of their communities, including meals where meat is served. In regards to emperor worship, Balaam could argue that Christians know that the emperor is a human being, not a god. Knowing that, the Christians should simply try to get along with the Romans and participate in the necessary rituals.

John, however, refuses to accept any accommodation to pagan ways. In John's understanding, Christians must avoid anything that compromises the faith. To eat meat offered to idols or to worship the emperor would to John's mind be a denial of Jesus Christ, and Christians simply cannot share in such actions.

Verse 15 continues with a warning not to hold to the teachings of the Nicolaitans. Most likely the Nicolaitans were a group in the church that was teaching the same thing as Balaam. The reading then continues with a call to repent, and the threat that if there is no repentance, Jesus will come in judgment. ("I will . . . make war against them with the sword of my mouth.") The congregation must reject its accommodation to pagan ways or face the judgment of Jesus!

Following this, there is the exhortation to listen to these words of the Spirit. The message concludes with a promise that those who conquer will be given hidden manna and a white stone with a new name on it. Hidden manna draws from the Old Testament food and points to the future heavenly feast. The white stone is most likely some kind of admission ticket to this future heavenly banquet.[6] Those who are faithful are promised the feast and joy of the heaven to come. Note the beauty of this promise. Those who are faithful to Christ will feast together with their Lord. They will share in the intimacy of Christ's presence; they will know and be known by their Lord. There is a heavenly banquet that awaits all who conquer!

The message to the congregation in Pergamum raises a powerful issue, the issue of accommodation to culture. When can Christians share in the ways of a sinful world, and when must Christians oppose those ways for the sake of Jesus? This will become a central issue in the book of Revelation. Moreover, this is an issue with which Christians must

[6] Caird, 42.

continually struggle. The church in every age (including ours!) must draw appropriate boundaries as to where it can share in the ways of the world, and where it must oppose those ways.

2:18-29

[18]"And to the angel of the church in Thyatira write: These are the words of the Son of God, who has eyes like a flame of fire, and whose feet are like burnished bronze:

[19]I know your works—Your love, faith, service, and patient endurance. I know that your last works are greater than the first. [20]But I have this against you: you tolerate that woman Jezebel, who calls herself a prophet and is teaching and beguiling my servants to practice fornication and to eat food sacrificed to idols. [21]I gave her time to repent, but she refuses to repent of her fornication. [22]Beware, I am throwing her on a bed, and those who commit adultery with her I am throwing into great distress, unless they repent of her doings; [23]and I will strike her children dead. And all the churches will know that I am the one who searches minds and hearts, and I will give to each of you as your works deserve. [24]But to the rest of you in Thyatira, who do not hold this teaching, who have not learned what some call 'the deep things of Satan,' to you I say, I do not lay on you any other burden; [25]only hold fast to what you have until I come. [26]To everyone who conquers and continues to do my works to the end, I will give authority over the nations; [27]to rule them with an iron rod, as when clay pots are shattered—[28]even as I also received authority from my Father. To the one who conquers I will also give the morning star. [29]Let anyone who has an ear listen to what the Spirit is saying to the churches.

Thyatira was a commercial city. It was home to many trades and trade guilds, including associations of potters, tailors, leather workers, linen workers, bakers, coppersmiths, dyers, slave dealers, bronzesmiths, and wool merchants.[7] Often these guilds would share dinners, which would include meat that had been offered to idols. Once again the Christians would have to struggle as to whether they could participate in the guilds and all that that meant.

After the greeting, the message begins with words of commendation, as this church is sharing in love, faith, service, and patient endurance. Not only is it sharing, it is growing in these things! But there is a problem. The congregation is tolerating a false prophetess that John labels as Jezebel. The original Jezebel was a queen of ancient Israel who promoted pagan worship and was opposed by the prophets Elijah and Elisha

---

[7] Metzger, 36.

(1 Kgs 18). John nicknames his opponent at Thyatira Jezebel as a way of labeling her as a false teacher. It seems that this Jezebel is teaching many of the same things as Balaam at Pergamum. John notes that she is teaching fornication, which could be sexual sins, but most likely refers to going after false gods as in emperor worship. She also allows the eating of food offered to idols. The problem is too much accommodation to the culture.

The situation at Thyatira is just the opposite of that of Ephesus. Ephesus has stayed doctrinally correct while losing love. Thyatira has maintained love, but has accepted false doctrines. John insists that the church must maintain both love and correct doctrine.

Jezebel and her followers are threatened with judgment, unless they repent. (The phrase "the deep things of Satan" is most likely a bit of sarcasm. Jezebel has probably been saying she teaches the "deep things of God," but John points out that her teaching is of Satan.[8]) John further points out that no extra burdens will be placed on the rest of the people at Thyatira, save that they hold fast to what they have.

Note the definition of prophecy that is being used here. Jezebel is accused of being a false prophetess. But there is no reference to her making inaccurate predictions about the future. What makes her a false prophetess is that she is incorrectly teaching people about the life of faith. As has been mentioned before, prophecy for John is about teaching and exhortation that leads people in faith.

The message ends with two promises. The first promise is that those who conquer will rule with Christ. The promise found in verses 26 and 27 is an echo of Psalm 2:9. (Psalm 2 was understood in Judaism as a "Messianic Psalm," a psalm that looked forward to the Messiah who would come and rule with a rod of iron. John draws from that understanding to promise that those who conquer will rule with Jesus who is the Messiah.) The second promise is that those who conquer will receive the morning star. This star is not a literal planet, of course. It is Christ himself, as we will learn in 22:16. Those who conquer will be given Jesus!

Chapter 3

3:1-6

"And to the angel of the church in Sardis write: These are the words of him who has the seven spirits of God and the seven stars:

---

[8] Koester, 62.

"I know your works; you have a name of being alive, but you are dead. [2]Wake up, and strengthen what remains and is on the point of death, for I have not found your works perfect in the sight of my God. [3]Remember then what you received and heard; obey it, and repent. If you do not wake up, I will come like a thief, and you will not know at what hour I will come to you. [4]Yet you have still a few persons in Sardis who have not soiled their clothes; they will walk with me, dressed in white, for they are worthy. [5]If you conquer, you will be clothed like them in white robes, and I will not blot your name out of the book of life; I will confess your name before my Father and before his angels. [6]Let anyone who has an ear listen to what the Spirit is saying to the churches.

Sardis was a commercial and industrial city. In previous centuries it had been a city of great wealth, including being home to the rich King Croesus in the sixth century B.C. By the time of Revelation, Sardis had lost some of its previous glory, but was still a city of prosperity and wealth.[9] Sardis had been destroyed by an earthquake in 17 A.D. and was rebuilt with Roman help. There were temples in Sardis to the goddess Artemis and Caesar Augustus. The oldest part of Sardis was built on a steep hill, which seemed to make the city safe from attack. However, twice in its history Sardis had fallen because of surprise attack and lack of watchfulness on the part of the guards. (John seems to refer to this history when he calls for watchfulness among the people.)

Jesus is introduced to Sardis by saying that he is the one "who has the seven spirits of God and the seven stars." Once again this introduction is rooted in the vision of chapter 1. Seven spirits, as was previously mentioned, refer to the spirits around the throne of God in Jewish thought, and perhaps the symbolism of seven is meant to imply the complete, full spirit of God. The seven stars in chapter 1 refer to angels. Jesus is the one who is filled with the Spirit of God and is Lord of the angels.

John goes on to point out that the church in Sardis has the reputation of being healthy and strong. But John accuses the Christians of actually being dead in the faith. He urges them to repent and return to what they had heard and received. The problem at Sardis is not persecution or assimilation with Roman culture. It is complacency. The church is comfortable, and doesn't seek a life transforming faith. The people are content to rest on their good reputations.

[9] Metzger, 38–39.

Jesus threatens to come like a thief in the night. This is not a reference to the Second Coming, but a conditional coming in judgment if the people do not repent. (Note that the coming of Jesus can refer to the Second Coming or it can refer to his coming among his people in the present. Jesus is a Lord who continuously comes to be with his people!) The congregation is urged to wake up in the faith.

There are a few in Sardis who are still faithful, and three promises are made to them and to those who will repent. First, they will wear white robes, a symbol of purity and victory. Second, they will not be blotted out of the book of life. Cities in ancient times kept a record of their citizens. Citizens could be "blotted out" as an announcement they have lost their citizenship and rights in the city. John warns the people of Sardis that if they do not repent, they will be blotted out of God's book of life, i.e., they will lose their citizenship in God's kingdom. Third, Jesus will confess those who are faithful before God and the angels.

The issue at Sardis is complacency, or perhaps even more, spiritual bankruptcy. A once healthy congregation has lost its faith. A good question to ask is, does the church at Sardis sound like any churches with which we are familiar? Are there modern churches with good reputations that are trying to live on that reputation, content to be comfortable? Christ continually calls congregations, and Christians, to a living, growing faith.

3:7-13

(7)"And to the angel of the church in Philadelphia write: These are the words of the holy one, the true one, who has the key of David, who opens and no one will shut, who shuts and no one opens:

8"I know your works. Look, I have set before you an open door, which no one is able to shut. I know that you have but little power, and yet you have kept my word and have not denied my name. 9I will make those of the synagogue of Satan who say that they are Jews and are not, but are lying—I will make them come and bow down before your feet, and they will learn that I have loved you. 10Because you have kept my word of patient endurance, I will keep you from the hour of trial that is coming on the whole world to test the inhabitants of the earth. 11I am coming soon; hold fast to what you have, so that no one may seize your crown. 12If you conquer, I will make you a pillar in the temple of my God; you will never go out of it. I will write on you the name of my God, and the name of the city of my God, the new Jerusalem that comes down from my God out of heaven, and my own new name. 13Let anyone who has an ear listen to what the Spirit is saying to the churches.

Philadelphia was the youngest of the seven cities addressed in Revelation. It had been founded in the second century B.C. by Attalus Philadelphos, a king of Pergamum.[10] The ancient historian Strabo called Philadelphia a "city full of earthquakes."[11] Earth tremors were common. A strong earthquake in 17 A.D. demolished Philadelphia, but the city had been rebuilt with the aid of the Romans.

John roots the message to Philadelphia in Jesus, but this time does not draw from the vision in chapter 1. John instead writes of the one who "has the key of David, who opens and no one will shut, who shuts and no one opens." This is a paraphrase of Isaiah 22:22, where a servant has the key to King David's house and determines who will enter the house. The words imply that Jesus is the one who is in the position to determine who will enter the kingdom of God.

The message to Philadelphia is one of commendation, with no censure. Jesus has set before the congregation an "open door," an open invitation to the kingdom that no one can shut. The congregation is said to have "but little power," most likely a reference that the congregation is small and poor. Like the congregation in Smyrna, this congregation is experiencing opposition from the local Jews. Yet this small congregation is faithful—"you have kept my word and not denied my name."

Jesus promises to keep this congregation "from the hour of trial that is coming on the whole world." Given what is said in the rest of the book of Revelation, this promise does not mean that these Christians will never experience suffering. It rather means that Christ will be with them and will sustain them even in the midst of suffering.

The message closes by saying that if the Christians conquer (i.e., are faithful), they will be made pillars in the temple of God and will have God's name and the name of the New Jerusalem written on them. This is a poetic way of saying that they will share in the salvation of God. It is a powerful image/promise. The Christians will bear the name of God and be built into the community of God!

3:14-22

[14]"And to the angel of the church in Laodicea write: The words of the Amen, the faithful and true witness, the origin of God's creation:

[15]"I know your works; you are neither cold nor hot. I wish that you were either cold or hot. [16]So, because you are lukewarm, and neither cold

[10] Metzger, 40.
[11] Ibid., 41.

nor hot, I am about to spit you out of my mouth. [17]For you say, 'I am rich, I have prospered, and I need nothing.' You do not realize that you are wretched, pitiable, poor, blind, and naked. [18]Therefore I counsel you to buy from me gold refined by fire so that you may be rich; and white robes to clothe you and to keep the shame of your nakedness from being seen; and salve to anoint your eyes so that you may see. [19]I reprove and discipline those whom I love. Be earnest, therefore, and repent. [20]Listen! I am standing at the door, knocking; if you hear my voice and open the door, I will come in to you and eat with you, and you with me. [21]To the one who conquers I will give a place with me on my throne, just as I myself conquered and sat down with my Father on his throne. [22]Let anyone who has an ear listen to what the Spirit is saying to the churches."

Laodicea was a prosperous commercial center in Asia Minor. The city was known as a banking center and for its textile industry, which included the production of a black wool. Laodicea also had a medical school that manufactured a well-known ear ointment. The city was destroyed by an earthquake in 60 A.D. and was rebuilt without the benefit of Roman aid.

This message begins by saying that Jesus is "the Amen, the faithful and true witness, the origin of God's creation." "Amen" comes from a Hebrew root that means strength and firmness.[12] John may be drawing here from Isaiah 65:16 where "God of Faithfulness" should be translated literally as "God of Amen."

The message to Laodicea is one of warning and condemnation. Jesus begins by pointing out, "I know your works, you are neither cold nor hot. I wish that you were either cold or hot. So because you are lukewarm, and neither cold nor hot, I am about to spit you out of my mouth." The congregation is accused of being lukewarm in faith, and that is unacceptable to Jesus. Note the harshness of these words. Jesus threatens to spit the congregation out of his mouth! (Stop and think about this imagery—What would it mean for Jesus to spit out his people?)

Jesus continues by pointing out that the congregation thinks they are "rich, prosperous, and need nothing." This is a self-confident congregation, content in their self-sufficiency and wealth. But their wealth has blinded them to the shallowness of their faith. Jesus then in pointed language calls the Christians back to himself. In fact, he calls them back in the terms of what makes their society strong. Instead of relying on

---

[12] Caird, 57.

the gold it brings in through its commercial center, he asks them to "buy from me gold refined by fire." Further, in place of their famous black wool, he invites them to buy white robes from him, and in place of the ointment for ears they produce, to buy from him "salve to anoint your eyes that you may see." The goods that the Laodiceans are counting on are nothing compared to the riches offered them by Christ.

John uses harsh language. This congregation is not nearly as healthy or faithful as it thinks it is. They think they are a model congregation, but in truth they are empty and must repent.[13]

The message ends, however, with a word of hope. Jesus points out that he reproves and disciplines those whom he loves. (There is a good reminder here for the modern church. Jesus does discipline his people, and we need to be open to that!) Moreover, in beautiful imagery, Jesus says he stands at the door knocking, and seeks to come in with the Laodiceans. The congregation is invited to open itself to the new life of Christ. The message closes with a promise, that those who conquer will be given a place with Jesus on his throne. The situation is bleak in Laodicea, but the congregation is invited back into the life of Christ.

Issues in the Seven Churches

Let's close chapters 2 and 3 with a question. What are the situations that John addresses in the book of Revelation? It is often said that Revelation is written as a word of hope for persecuted Christians. That is true, but it is not the whole story. Revelation, rather, is written to address three specific issues.

1. There is the problem of persecution. The churches at Smyrna and Philadelphia faced opposition from the Jews and Romans. At Pergamum, Antipas was killed for the faith. There is persecution, and John foresees more to come. We need also remember, however, that there was not a widespread or systematic persecution of Christians at this time in history.

---

[13] Some scholars think that John is drawing from the local situation to make his point. Scholars like Colin Hemer in *The Letters to the Seven Churches of Asia in Their Local Setting* (pp. 178–209) argue that the reference to water refers to the local water supply. The nearby city of Hierapolis had natural hot springs, while another nearby city, Colassae, had natural cold water. Laodicea's water would have been lukewarm. Likewise Hemer argues that the gold refined by fire is a reference to the banking business in Laodicea, the white robes a reference to the textile industry, and the eye salve a reference to the medical school. Recent scholarship by Craig Koester and others has called this interpretation into question, and suggests that the references are instead examples from everyday life. Either way John's point is clear—the church in Laodicea is shallow and lacking in faith.

There was some persecution, and John foresaw more coming. But it was not an all-encompassing thing for the seven churches.

Revelation is written as a message of hope for churches that face persecution. It is the assurance that Jesus is the ultimate ruler of all creation, and that Jesus will triumph over all that can oppress God's people. This message of hope continues to speak to Christians throughout the ages. Christians can dare to trust in the justice and victory of Jesus.

2. There is the problem of accommodation to Roman ways. For the churches in Pergamum, Thyatira, and Ephesus, the main problem is that the congregations are tempted to embrace too many Roman practices. The issues of meat sacrificed to idols and emperor worship are the main issues here. The underlying question is one of assimilation, of accommodation. How much can the church accept of the ways of an unfaithful world?

Revelation is a message of warning and exhortation for congregations that look to accommodate themselves to unfaithful ways. It is a call for obedience and patient endurance on the part of Christians, even when that means standing against the ways of the world. The warnings in Revelation serve to direct Christians away from false practices, and back to obedience to Jesus Christ.

3. There is the problem of complacency. The churches in Sardis and Laodicea have become complacent, comfortable. Their problem is not with persecution. Quite the contrary, they are content in their situation and comfortable in a shallow faith.

Revelation is written as a wake-up call for complacent Christians. It is the challenge for comfortable congregations to seek a living, active faith. Once again, the warnings in the book serve to direct Christians back to a life of obedience.

Revelation was written to address a variety of situations in first century Asia Minor. These issues, and related forms of these issues, have continued to affect Christians throughout history. John's words spoke powerfully to Christians in first century Asia Minor and they have spoken powerfully throughout the life of the church. These words continue to speak powerfully today as we modern Christians find ourselves faced with similar challenges.

Section III
In the Throne Room
Chapters 4–5

With chapter 4 John begins a major new portion of the book. John now finds himself in the midst of the heavenly throne room. As you read this section, note the sheer grandeur of God and his heavenly court. Even more, note how John is insisting that at the center of this entire cosmos is God. It is God who is the center of all things, the source and goal of life, the Almighty One!

Chapter 4

As we move from chapter 3 to chapter 4, we move through one of the major transitions in the book. The messages to the seven churches are completed. Now the scene shifts from earth to heaven.

4:1-6a

After this I looked, and there in heaven a door stood open! And the first voice, which I had heard speaking to me like a trumpet, said, "Come up here, and I will show you what must take place after this." [2]At once I was in the spirit, and there in heaven stood a throne, with one seated on the throne! [3]And the one seated there looks like jasper and carnelian, and around the throne is a rainbow that looks like an emerald. [4]Around the throne are twenty-four thrones, and seated on the thrones are twenty-four elders, dressed in white robes, with golden crowns on their heads. [5]Coming from the throne are flashes of lightning, and rumblings and peals of thunder, and in front of the throne burn seven flaming torches, which are the seven spirits of God; [6]and in front of the throne there is something like a sea of glass, like crystal.

John looks and sees in heaven an open door. The first voice that he has heard, i.e. Jesus, now says, "Come up here, and I will show you what must take place after this." Note the linkage that John provides with the message to the church in Laodicea. To the church in Laodicea, Christ says he "stands at the door and knocks." The question is, will the church open the door to Christ? Now this same Christ opens heaven's door to the churches, through the message of John.[1]

John once again notes that he was "in the spirit" (compare to 1:10). In the spirit he is taken to heaven, where he sees a throne. Not only does he see a throne, but One seated on it. These words make a powerful and pointed proclamation. At the center of the universe is a throne! This world is not left to chaos; it is not a hopeless mishmash of events. There is a throne and a ruler; there is a purpose! Moreover, the throne is not occupied by the Roman emperor. Nor is it surrounded by American flags. It is occupied by God. At the center of the universe is God and God alone!

---

[1] Craig Koester, *Revelation and the End of All Things* (Grand Rapids: Wm. Eerdmans Publishing Co., 2001), 71.

John goes on to use picturesque language to describe this heavenly scene. Much of John's description of the heavenly throne room is taken from the first chapter of Ezekiel, with one important difference. Unlike Ezekiel, John doesn't describe God in human terms. John rather says that the one on the throne "looks like jasper and carnelian." These are precious, shining gems, which suggest the glory of God. John then adds, "around the throne is a rainbow that looks like an emerald." The best way to deal with this imagery is to simply let our imaginations run with it. Try to imagine a rainbow that looks like an emerald. John is stretching our imaginations and doing so to proclaim the sheer majesty of God.

Around the throne are twenty-four elders, with each on a throne. The elders are dressed in white robes with golden crowns, i.e., they are pictured as royalty. What is being developed here is a picture of the heavenly court, with God at the center. Why are there twenty-four elders? We aren't sure. Perhaps they represent an Old Testament council of angels. Perhaps the twenty-four is reached by adding the twelve sons of Jacob in Israel's history with the twelve apostles. Once again the point is one of majesty and power.

Coming from the throne are flashes of lightning and peals of thunder. They remind us of the power and the danger of God. In addition there are seven flaming torches, which are identified as the seven spirits of God. Before the throne is a sea of glass, like crystal. The sea of glass might be a reference to Solomon's temple, where a molten sea is mentioned in 1 Kings 7:23. Or perhaps John is drawing on some Old Testament symbolism, where the sea is often a symbol of chaos. But here, in heaven, the sea (and chaos) is overcome. It is smooth as glass.

The best way to appreciate this imagery is to stop and recognize the sheer grandeur of it. Perhaps we as readers ought not focus so much on analyzing this picture, but simply step back and see the wonder and majesty of it. John is giving us powerful images of God, and he paints word pictures to do so. The proclamation is of the majesty, the wonder, the magnificence of our Creator!

One of the questions that is often asked about Revelation is why does John use all these symbols and imageries? Couldn't he just tell us things directly? Here we see an answer to that. John paints word pictures, pictures that overwhelm our minds. His images create feelings and associations; they set our imaginations ringing. In the process he gives us a sense of the sheer grandeur of God.

4:6b-11

Around the throne, and on each side of the throne, are four living creatures, full of eyes in front and behind: [7]the first living creature like a lion, the second living creature like an ox, the third living creature with a face like a human face, and the fourth living creature like a flying eagle. [8]And the four living creatures, each of them with six wings, are full of eyes all around and inside. Day and night without ceasing they sing, "Holy, holy, holy, the Lord God the Almighty, who was and is and is to come." [9]And whenever the living creatures give glory and honor and thanks to the one who is seated on the throne, who lives forever and ever, [10]the twenty-four elders fall before the one who is seated on the throne and worship the one who lives forever and ever; they cast their crowns before the throne, singing, [11]"You are worthy, our Lord and God, to receive glory and honor and power, for you created all things, and by your will they existed and were created."

John now writes that around the throne are four living creatures. They are full of eyes, which indicate they are all-seeing. (God knows what is going on in His creation!) These living creatures are like a lion, an ox, a third with a face like a human, and a flying eagle, imagery also found in a vision in Ezekiel 1. What John is proclaiming is that around the throne of God are representatives of all creation. God is God of all the world, and all the world is to be directed to God.

These four living creatures have six wings. Here John is drawing from a heavenly scene in Isaiah 6:2. Isaiah wrote of six-winged seraphim, heavenly creatures, that stood before the throne of God and praised God. It was an Old Testament image of the grandeur of the heavenly court. John draws on this and writes that the four living creatures praise God. Day and night the living creatures sing, "Holy, holy, holy, the Lord God the Almighty, who was and is and is to come." The point is that all of creation is involved in the worship of God.

When the living creatures worship, the twenty-four elders fall and cast their crowns before the throne. This is a sign of obedience, and has parallels in how kings would offer a sign of obedience to the Roman emperor. (Once again John's not-so-subtle point is that ultimate obedience is due to God and not the emperor.) The chapter ends with all the heavenly court joining to praise and worship the God who is the source of all things.

Comments on Chapter 4

A few observations on chapter 4 need to be underscored. First, notice how this new part of Revelation (which will include most of the rest of the book) begins in God and in the worship of God. What is central for Revelation, what is central for creation, is Almighty God. Too often Revelation is seen as a book of only judgment and destruction. We do well to observe how John begins the heavenly vision with the glory and wonder of God.

Second, Revelation is thoroughly rooted in worship. The heavenly vision begins with a magnificent scene of worship. Moreover, Revelation will return to worship again and again. One of the messages of Revelation is that we are to be a people of worship.

Third, as we deal with both chapters 4 and 5, we do well to step back and see the sheer majesty of God. Perhaps the most appropriate thing we can do as we seek to appreciate Revelation is to join in the choir and praise God!

Chapter 5

5:1-5

Then I saw in the right hand of the one seated on the throne a scroll written on the inside and on the back, sealed with seven seals; [2]and I saw a mighty angel proclaiming with a loud voice, "Who is worthy to open the scroll and break its seals?" [3]And no one in heaven or on earth or under the earth was able to open the scroll or to look into it. [4]And I began to weep bitterly because no one was found worthy to open the scroll or to look into it. [5]Then one of the elders said to me, "Do not weep. See, the Lion of the tribe of Judah, the Root of David, has conquered, so that he can open the scroll and its seven seals."

John sees in the hand of God a scroll, written on both the inside and the back. This scroll is sealed with seven seals. (A seal was a piece of wax on the edge of a scroll, usually inscribed with a ring imprint. The seal served to guarantee the truth and validity of the message.) This scroll contains God's plan for the world. As we will see, opening the seals puts this plan into motion.

But there is a problem. A mighty angel asks, "Who is worthy to open the scroll and break its seals?" In other words, who is able to bring about God's redemption for the world? No one is worthy and John weeps.

There is a point here worth underscoring. None of us are worthy or able to bring about God's redemption or newness for this world of sin. Left to ourselves we are without hope.

One of the elders speaks to John. He says, "Do not weep. See, the Lion of the tribe of Judah, the Root of David, has conquered, so that he can open the scroll and its seven seals." There is one who can deliver this world, and us! This one is described in Old Testament images for the Messiah. The Old Testament expected that God would send a messianic warrior king who would save the people. This Messiah would be a "Lion from the tribe of Judah," who would conquer by killing and defeating the enemies of Israel. In addition this Messiah would be the "Root of David," a descendant of the great Old Testament king. This one will open the seals and bring about God's plan.

5:6-7

[6]Then I saw between the throne and the four living creatures and among the elders a Lamb standing as if it had been slaughtered, having seven horns and seven eyes, which are the seven spirits of God sent out into all the earth. [7]He went and took the scroll from the right hand of the one who is seated on the throne.

We come now to an incredible change of images. John has been promised a Lion, but what comes is a Lamb! (In fact, note John *hears* about a Lion, but he *sees* a Lamb.[2] This distinction will become important in chapter 7.) This is an incredible, stark change of images! A few comments are in order:

1. The Lamb, of course, is Jesus. From now on in the book the image of the Lamb becomes the dominant image for Jesus.

2. This change of image from Lion to Lamb is not to be seen as a contradiction. Nor is it a denial of the Old Testament promises and expectations. Quite the contrary, in the wisdom of God, all the Old Testament promises and expectations for the Lion are fulfilled by the Lamb.

3. John's imagery here ought to make us think of Palm Sunday. The crowds on Palm Sunday turned out to welcome the warrior king who would fight off the Romans. Instead they met the Lord who rode in on a donkey and died as a servant. John's change of images here is rooted in the ministry of Jesus.

---

[2] Richard Bauckham, *The Theology of the Book of Revelation* (Cambridge: Cambridge University Press, 1993), 74.

4. Incredibly, this Lamb does conquer. But the Lamb conquers not by killing his enemies, but by dying for his enemies. (The symbol of the Lamb for Jesus raises all sorts of connections with sacrifice and the Passover.) This Lamb overcomes God's enemies, yes, but he does so by the cross!

John moves on to tell us about the Lamb. The Lamb has been slaughtered; he is the crucified one. The Lamb has horns, a horn being a symbol of royal power (Psalm 132:17). This Lamb has seven horns, symbolizing complete power! The Lamb also has seven eyes, which John explains as the seven spirits of God sent into all the earth. This imagery points to the Lamb as all-seeing, and filled with the divine spirit. The Lamb now takes the scroll from the hand of God.

5:8-14

[8]When he had taken the scroll, the four living creatures and the twenty-four elders fell before the Lamb, each holding a harp and golden bowls full of incense, which are the prayers of the saints. [9]They sing a new song: "You are worthy to take the scroll and to open its seals, for you were slaughtered and by your blood you ransomed for God saints from every tribe and language and people and nation; [10]you have made them to be a kingdom and priests serving our God, and they will reign on earth."

[11]Then I looked, and I heard the voice of many angels surrounding the throne and the living creatures and the elders; they numbered myriads of myriads and thousands of thousands, [12]singing with full voice, "Worthy is the Lamb that was slaughtered to receive power and wealth and wisdom and might and honor and glory and blessing!" [13]Then I heard every creature in heaven and on earth and under the earth and in the sea, and all that is in them, singing, "To the one seated on the throne and to the Lamb be blessing and honor and glory and might forever and ever!" [14]And the four living creatures said, "Amen!" And the elders fell down and worshiped.

As the Lamb takes the scroll, an incredible scene of worship begins. They sing a new song, proclaiming that the Lamb is worthy to open the scroll, for the Lamb has been slaughtered and by its blood has ransomed people for God. The proclamation is that Jesus is the one who fulfills all the plans and purposes of God.

Comments on Chapter 5

Two additional comments need to be made on chapter 5. First, the Lamb does not replace God. The Lamb rather joins God at the throne and as the center of worship. The Lamb is the means by which God works out his purposes for the world.

Second, as was noted in chapter 4, this heavenly vision is rooted in worship. The entire book is rooted in worship. We will need that foundation as we approach what is to come next.

Section IV

Seven Seals

Chapters 6:1–8:2

In this section the scene shifts from the glories of heavenly worship to catastrophic events on the earth. The seals on the scroll are opened one by one, and each seal unleashes incredible trauma. Watch how the opening of these seals is meant to unsettle us and shatter any sense of security that is not rooted in God.

Chapter 6

In this chapter the first six of the seals on the scroll are opened. As each of the six is opened, there is a message of threat or worry. Too often we think that we do not need to take God seriously. Chapter 6 is meant to shake us out of that. We begin with the four horsemen, as the first four seals are opened.

6:1-2

Then I saw the Lamb open one of the seven seals, and I heard one of the four living creatures call out, as with a voice of thunder, "Come!" ²I looked, and there was a white horse! Its rider had a bow; a crown was given to him, and he came out conquering and to conquer.

The first seal is opened, and one of the living creatures calls out "Come!" A rider comes, mounted on a white horse. He has a bow and a crown and he comes out to conquer. (This imagery of horsemen and colored horses is drawn from Zechariah, although John dramatically reworks the imagery.) A mounted archer would make the people of first-century Asia think of the Parthians. The Parthian Empire was the empire that bordered the eastern edge of the Roman Empire. The Romans could not subdue the Parthians. In fact, in the century that preceded the writing of Revelation, the Romans had been defeated by the Parthians a number of times. The Roman Empire lived with a fear of a Parthian invasion. (For modern similarities to this, we might think in terms of the "Red Menace," the Russian threat during the Cold War. Or in the twenty-first century, we ought to think in terms of a terrorist strike.) This mounted archer would suggest the Parthians and the fear involved with their threat.

6:3-4

³When he opened the second seal, I heard the second living creature call out, "Come!" ⁴And out came another horse, bright red; its rider was permitted to take peace from the earth, so that people would slaughter one another, and he was given a great sword.

The second seal is opened, and a horseman on a bright red horse comes. He is given a great sword. This horseman takes peace from the earth, so that people would slaughter each other. The message is of violence and fear.

6:5-6

[5]When he opened the third seal, I heard the third living creature call out, "Come!" I looked, and there was a black horse! Its rider held a pair of scales in his hand, [6]and I heard what seemed to be a voice in the midst of the four living creatures saying, "A quart of wheat for a day's pay, and three quarts of barley for a day's pay, but do not damage the olive oil and the wine!"

The third seal is opened and a horseman comes on a black horse. He carries a pair of scales. This horseman wreaks economic hardship on the earth. "A quart of wheat for a day's pay" means that the economy is in turmoil. How long could people survive or feed their families under those circumstances? People might survive for a while, but soon their situations would become desperate. And yet the voice also announces, "Do not harm the olive oil and the wine." The luxury items do just fine. The imagery suggests that in times of economic turmoil, the poor suffer and the rich continue to live in comfort.

6:7-8

[7]When he opened the fourth seal, I heard the voice of the fourth living creature call out, "Come!" [8]I looked and there was a pale green horse! Its rider's name was Death, and Hades followed with him; they were given authority over a fourth of the earth, to kill with sword, famine, and pestilence, and by the wild animals of the earth.

The fourth seal is opened and a fourth horseman comes out. He rides a horse of a sickly, ghastly green color. This horseman is identified as Death. Death and Hades are given authority to kill one-quarter of the earth's population.

What is John saying with these images? What John is doing is shaking the sense of security of Christians in first century Asia Minor.[1] Try to imagine how this message would sound in first century Laodicea.

---

[1] The following ideas are taken from Craig Koester's book, *Revelation and the End of All Things*, p. 81 and following.

Laodicea was the rich, self-sufficient congregation. They have most likely made their peace with Roman ways; they are content in their own security. This is the *Pax Romana* in ancient history, a time to depend on Rome for growth and protection. The Christians in Laodicea are content and secure. But now John says, "Wait a minute. Are you really as secure as you think?" With each horseman John systematically pricks the Christians' sense of security.

Horseman 1—Do you think you are secure? What about the Parthians off to your east? Rome can't subdue them. What happens if the Parthians invade?

Horseman 2—How safe are you in terms of violence in your community? The second horseman and his sword reminds you that there is violence and threat even in the midst of your own town.

Horseman 3—How about the economy? Are you sure it is stable? Do you know for sure that you will have enough to survive? Will you be able to support your family?

Horseman 4—Finally, even if you can escape all the rest, what about death? Sooner or later you will deal with your own mortality.

The Christians thought they could be secure without a deep devotion to God. So, John says, let's see how secure you are. The horsemen are meant to remind people of how tenuous life really is.

Let's go one step further with this, and ask how John's imagery might apply to our contemporary situation. As modern day American Christians, perhaps even more than first century Christians, we try to find our security in ourselves. Our day is sometimes called the *Pax Americana.* We think we are safe and secure. Too often we don't concern ourselves with directing our lives to God, for we see ourselves as self-sufficient. But John's words challenge us.

Horseman 1—Are we really safe in America? If we are looking for ultimate security in our nation, can we guarantee it? Remember September 11, 2001? Our sense of security has forever been shaken and we realize we aren't as secure as we thought.

Horseman 2—How about violence in our society? Our news reports are full of stories of murder and violence and drugs. Is it safe to walk all the streets in your town?

Horseman 3—What about economics? Are we really as prosperous as we think? In the late 1990s, it seemed that everyone was making money in the stock market. That's not the case now. How secure is your job and your retirement?

Horseman 4—If you can somehow escape all of the above, what about death? Did the last funeral you went to make you feel uneasy? Though we try to deny it, our own mortality is all too close.

When we read Revelation, we should think about our own sense of security. We tend to think we can build a life without God. John is digging away at that notion. He presents us with threats to remind us that true security cannot be found in the things of this world.

6:9-11

⁹When he opened the fifth seal, I saw under the altar the souls of those who had been slaughtered for the word of God and for the testimony they had given; ¹⁰they cried out with a loud voice, "Sovereign Lord, holy and true, how long will it be before you judge and avenge our blood on the inhabitants of the earth?" ¹¹They were each given a white robe and told to rest a little longer, until the number would be complete both of their fellow servants and of their brothers and sisters, who were soon to be killed as they themselves had been killed.

The pattern now shifts with the fifth seal. John sees an altar, a heavenly altar. Under the altar are the souls of those who have been slaughtered for the word of God and for their testimony to it. John is clear—there will be persecution and even death for Christians because of their faith.

These martyred Christians have a question: Lord, how long before you judge the earth and avenge our blood? Some readers of Revelation have said that this sentiment is not worthy of Christians. True Christians, the argument goes, would not cry out for vengeance. To answer that, we need to note that this is a natural question, and a very real reaction to suffering and death. Moreover, what is behind the question is a cry for justice. God, if you are a God of justice, you have to do something about the slaughter of your people!

These slaughtered witnesses are given a white robe (a symbol of purity and victory) and told to wait "until the number would be complete of their fellow servants who were to be killed." This is an ominous statement. There will be more persecutions to come. Note also, the martyrs are not given a direct answer to their question. The question they are asking is a good one. It is a question of why God permits suffering, and how God can allow evil to triumph. The question is not answered at this point. Just a word of reference, the question will be answered later in Revelation. For now we are to hold on to it.

John also points out that the souls are located "under the altar." That is deliberate wording on John's part. In the sacrifices of ancient Israel, the blood of sacrificed animals was thrown at the altar, and would run under the altar. Blood was understood to symbolize life; as such the sacrifice would literally be "under the altar." What John is saying when he says that the souls are under the altar is that these Christians who died were sacrifices to God. Their deaths were not some meaningless travesty of justice. Quite the contrary, in their faithful witness they have become sacrifices to the Almighty. Note how John is reversing the earthly view here. From the earthly perspective, Christians who were killed were simply hapless victims before a Roman court of law. But from the heavenly perspective, God reverses all that. The Christians were not hapless victims, but sacrifices to God!

One additional comment needs to be made on these first five seals. One of the questions we ask of Revelation is, when will these things happen? We wonder if the book is referring only to things in the past, or is a prediction of future events. We do better to realize that these events have happened, are happening, and will continue to happen. With the first four seals, John is shaking Christians' sense of security by reminding them of ongoing threats. Those threats were real in the first century, they are real today, and will continue to be real as long as this earth endures. Likewise the fifth seal is a warning of persecution. That was a real threat in the first century. It is still a threat today. (As a point of fact, more Christians were killed for the faith in the twentieth century than in any other.) Revelation is best read not by trying to put these events on some neat timeline, but rather by asking how these words function in the life of faith. These words call us (and Christians of all centuries) away from earthly securities and back to the God who alone provides true security.

6:12-17

[12]When he opened the sixth seal, I looked, and there came a great earthquake; the sun became black as sackcloth, the full moon became like blood, [13]and the stars of the sky fell to the earth as the fig tree drops its winter fruit when shaken by a gale. [14]The sky vanished like a scroll rolling itself up, and every mountain and island was removed from its place. [15]Then the kings of the earth and the magnates and the generals and the rich and the powerful, and everyone, slave and free, hid in the caves and among the rocks of the mountains, [16]calling to the mountains and rocks, "Fall on us and hide us from the face of the one seated on the throne and from the wrath of the Lamb; [17]for the great day of their wrath has come, and who is able to stand?"

The sixth seal is opened and there is a cosmic shaking. There is a great earthquake (the people in ancient Asia Minor would have been able to relate to that), the sun becomes black, the moon becomes like blood, the stars fall to the earth, and the sky vanishes. Mountains and islands are removed and people great and small hide themselves.

This is language of judgment. John is drawing this language from the Old Testament prophets (for example, Isa 34:4, Joel 2:30-31, Amos 8:9). Peter uses similar language to describe the first Pentecost in Acts 2:19-20. This language functions symbolically, as is the case throughout Revelation. (For example, what would it literally mean for the moon to become like blood, or the sky to be rolled up like a scroll?) The language here announces judgment. When people refuse to listen to God, they will answer for that!

John uses this language as a word of warning, a warning to live lives of faith and obedience. Moreover, John is sharing a specific message here for the seven churches. One of the temptations the churches faced was to try to find their security by compromising their faith with Roman ways. John announces here that Roman society, and society as a whole, will face the judgment of God. The Christians are reminded not to compromise with that which ultimately will be destroyed.

Verse 15 goes further and points out that people, both great and small, try to hide from the Lamb. This is intriguing; the people do not repent. In the face of judgment the people hide rather than repent and return to God.

All of this language of judgment raises a question for twenty-first century Christians. Does God indeed judge? We live in an age that tends to say no. In the modern church, God is often seen as a benevolent grandfather who would never challenge anyone. But that is not the Biblical God. God's will, as expressed in Revelation and throughout the Bible, is not only to rescue his faithful people from an unfaithful creation. God's will is rather to reclaim all of creation. God is sovereign, and he will reclaim his world. To that end God will "destroy the destroyers of the earth." As God reclaims his world, he will judge all that will not return to him.

It needs to be stressed that God's deepest desire is that all people return to him. All through the book of Revelation, even in scenes of judgment, there will be many, many opportunities for repentance. (In fact, one of the goals of judgment language in Revelation is to lead people to repentance. One of the functions of these warnings is to drive people, including us, back to God.) But the book is also clear that if evil will not repent, it will be destroyed as God brings about the new heaven and new earth.

Chapter 6 ends with a question. "Who can stand?" Given all the warnings in chapter 6, given all the words of threat and judgment, can anyone stand? This question serves as a bridge into chapter 7, which will answer the question.

Chapter 7

7:1-3

After this I saw four angels standing at the four corners of the earth, holding back the four winds of the earth so that no wind could blow on earth or sea or against any tree. ²I saw another angel ascending from the rising of the sun, having the seal of the living God, and he called with a loud voice to the four angels who had been given power to damage earth and sea, ³saying, "Do not damage the earth or the sea or the trees, until we have marked the servants of our God with a seal on their foreheads."

John sees four angels at the four corners of the earth, holding back the winds. They are holding back the destruction. This serves to announce an interlude in the judgment. After all the intensity of chapter 6, we are here given a break.

Another angel comes and announces, "Do not damage the earth or the sea or the trees, until we have marked the servants of our God with a seal on their foreheads." To be sealed (or marked with a seal) is to belong to God. It is to be identified as God's servant, and as one protected by God. We ought not to think of a literal mark, but rather of God's claim on the person. Perhaps we ought to hear echoes of baptism here, as in baptism we are sealed in the Spirit of God. (In Revelation, evil will often parody God and try to look like God. Here we are told that the followers of God are sealed. Later in the book the followers of Satan will be marked.)

The damage/judgment of the last chapter is stopped until the servants of God are sealed. Who can stand in the face of destruction and threat? Those who are sealed, who belong to God! In God's care they will withstand all that will come. Chapter 7 is a message of assurance that God's people will be cared for in all that happens.

7:4-12

[4]And I heard the number of those who were sealed, one hundred forty-four thousand, sealed out of every tribe of the people of Israel: [5]From the tribe of Judah twelve thousand sealed, from the tribe of Reuben twelve thousand, from the tribe of Gad twelve thousand, [6]from the tribe of Asher twelve thousand, from the tribe of Naphtali twelve thousand, from the tribe of Manasseh twelve thousand, [7]from the tribe of Simeon twelve thousand, from the tribe of Levi twelve thousand, from the tribe of Issachar twelve thousand, [8]from the tribe of Zebulun twelve thousand, from the tribe of Joseph twelve thousand, from the tribe of Benjamin twelve thousand sealed.

[9]After this I looked, and there was a great multitude that no one could count, from every nation, from all tribes and peoples and languages, standing before the throne and before the Lamb, robed in white, with palm branches in their hands. [10]They cried out in a loud voice, saying, "Salvation belongs to our God who is seated on the throne, and to the Lamb!" [11]And all the angels stood around the throne and around the elders and the four living creatures, and they fell on their faces before the throne and worshipped God, [12]singing, "Amen! Blessing and glory and wisdom and thanksgiving and honor and power and might be to our God forever and ever! Amen."

John now shares two visions of those who are sealed. First John hears that 144,000 people from the tribes of Israel are sealed. This number should not be taken literally. The number 144,000—or 12 times 12 times 1000—indicates completeness. The image here points to the faithfulness of God to his Old Testament promises. In the Old Testament, God had promised to save Israel. These verses announce that God will save the complete number from Israel. (Again, be careful about taking this passage too literally. As point of fact, the twelve tribes of Israel hadn't existed for hundreds of years prior to John's writing. The tribes could not be found to gather people out of them!) Rather than a literal counting of Israelites, this passage is a symbolic way of speaking of God's faithfulness to all his promises of old.

Beginning in verse 9, John shares a second vision of those who are sealed. This time the vision is of a great multitude. Here the multitude of people that are sealed is too great even to count. They are from every tribe and language and nation. They wave palm branches and are clothed in white, symbols of victory.

How do we reconcile these two visions of those who are sealed/ saved? Will 144,000 Israelites be saved, or a great multitude from all nations, a multitude that is too great to count? Richard Bauckham has a helpful insight here. That is, these two visions point to the same reality.[2] John is doing the same thing here that he did in chapters 4 and 5. In chapters 4 and 5 John *heard* a lion (the Old Testament promise), and he *saw* a Lamb (the fulfillment in Christ). John lifted up the Old Testament promise, but pointed to an even greater fulfillment in Christ. Now in this chapter, John does the same thing. John *hears* 144,000 from Israel (the Old Testament promise), and he *sees* a great multitude (the fulfillment in Christ). John is once again saying that God is faithful to all his Old Testament promises. But the fulfillment of the promises in Christ will be even greater than Israel expected, as multitudes of people are saved.

John then goes on to point out that this multitude of the redeemed worships God. In fact the multitude is joined by the whole heavenly court in wonderful worship. Note how the book of Revelation has returned to worship. This passage sounds like chapters 4 and 5, as the heavens erupt in songs of praises.

7:13-17

[13]Then one of the elders addressed me, saying, "Who are these, robed in white, and where have they come from?" [14]I said to him, "Sir, you are the one that knows." Then he said to me, "These are they who have come out of the great ordeal; they have washed their robes and made them white in the blood of the Lamb. [15]For this reason they are before the throne of God, and worship him day and night within his temple, and the one who is seated on the throne will shelter them. [16]They will hunger no more, and thirst no more; the sun will not strike them, nor any scorching heat; [17]for the Lamb at the center of the throne will be their shepherd, and he will guide them to springs of the water of life, and God will wipe away every tear from their eyes."

One of the elders now explains to John who these people in the great multitude are. They are the ones who have come out of the great ordeal. (Note the implication of suffering to come.) They have been faithful even in the face of suffering and persecution and now celebrate in God's victory. Moreover, they have washed their robes in the blood of the Lamb and made them white. (Once again do not take this image literally. Robes can't be washed in blood to make them white. But the point is clear—these people have been saved by the blood of Jesus!)

---

[2] Richard Bauckham, *The Theology of the Book of Revelation* (Cambridge: Cambridge University Press, 1993), 76.

The chapter ends with promises for the multitude, promises that God will take care of his people. These promises are for the most part drawn from the Old Testament. The people will be constantly with God (Ezek 37:27). They will not hunger or thirst nor be struck by the sun (Isa 49:10). God will wipe away every tear (Isa 25:8). These are wonderful, tender promises of the care of God.

Comments on Chapter 7

Three comments on chapter 7 are helpful.

First, chapter 7 has answered the question of chapter 6. Chapter 6 ended by asking, who can stand? The answer is, those who have been redeemed/sealed by the Lamb! In fact, note how chapter 6 takes away all earthly security, but chapter 7 comes back to assure us that ultimate security is found in God.[3]

Second, chapter 7 provides a break, an interlude in the scenes of judgment. Chapter 6 is judgment, chapters 8 and 9 are judgment. We need this break in chapter 7!

Third, watch how Revelation returns again and again to worship.

Chapter 8

8:1-2

When the Lamb opened the seventh seal, there was silence in heaven for about half an hour. [2]And I saw the seven angels who stand before God, and seven trumpets were given to them.

The interlude is completed, and John now returns to the seals. In the opening verse of chapter 8, the seventh and final seal is opened. We might expect that with the seventh seal, we would come to the end. In the sixth seal, the earth has been judged. The cosmos itself has been shaken. We would expect now the coming of God and the end of the story. But that is not what happens. The seventh seal is opened and there is—silence! There is silence in heaven for half an hour.

An interesting question is how would you imagine this silence? We do well to think in terms of an awesome, powerful, holy silence. This is silence in the presence of the Almighty. "Be still and know that I am God"

---

[3] Koester, 91.

(Ps 46:10). It is the profound silence of being in the presence of the Creator.

Following the half hour of silence, seven trumpets are brought out and given to seven angels. These trumpets will be blown to introduce a new series of plagues. Rather than being at the end of the story, we are about to start a new series of judgment.

This is a good place to reassert a key concept in approaching Revelation. That is, the book does not proceed in chronological fashion. There is rather a repetition in the book as John returns to and redevelops ideas that have been previously presented. For example, with the seventh seal, we should be finishing the book. But the opening of the seventh seal leads instead into a new series, the seven trumpets. There is a repetition, a recapitulation going on.

In fact to underscore this point, notice how John includes details that make it impossible to read Revelation in chronological fashion. In 8:7 all the green grass will be destroyed. But in 9:4 the locust are instructed not to harm the green grass. In 6:13 the stars fall to the earth. In 8:12 the stars are back in the sky in order to fall again. It is as if John is reminding us not to read this in a linear fashion. There is a repetition, an intensifying of the message. Perhaps we ought to think of Revelation in terms of a hymn, with a repetition of verses and refrains as the message is sounded again and again.

The seven seals have been opened. Judgment has followed. As we continue onward in Revelation, there is more judgment to come!

Section V

The Seven Trumpets

Chapters 8:3–9:20

Seven trumpets are now sounded. The trumpets announce a new series of judgment which is more intense than the last. The escalating scenes of judgment pound away at our imaginations. Yet this section ends with the stark note that even with all this, humankind still refuses to turn to God.

Chapter 8

8:3-6

³Another angel with a golden censer came and stood at the altar; he was given a great quantity of incense to offer with the prayers of all the saints on the golden altar that is before the throne. ⁴And the smoke of the incense, with the prayers of the saints, rose before God from the hand of the angel. ⁵Then the angel took the censer and filled it with fire from the altar and threw it on the earth; and there were peals of thunder, rumblings, flashes of lightning, and an earthquake. ⁶Now the seven angels who had the seven trumpets made ready to blow them.

As John transitions from the seven seals to the seven trumpets, he notes that an angel comes to the heavenly altar. John reports how the angel mingles the prayers of the saints with incense, and the prayers and the incense rise before God. John will use this imagery a number of times in the book. It is a high view of prayer, a powerful reminder that our prayers do rise to the very presence of God. Perhaps we should also make a connection here with 6:9-11, where the saints have prayed for God to act against evil. Now with the seven trumpets, God will do precisely that. Perhaps the actions of this next section are God's response to the prayers of the saints.

Following the prayers, the angel takes fire from the altar and throws it on the earth. There is thunder, lightning, and a shaking of the earth. This serves to announce the plagues that are about to come. The passage concludes with the seven angels now ready to blow the trumpets.

8:7

⁷The first angel blew his trumpet, and there came hail and fire, mixed with blood, and they were hurled to the earth; and a third of the earth was burned up, and a third of the trees were burned up, and all green grass was burned up.

An angel blows the first trumpet and hail and fire and blood are hurled to the earth. This destruction recalls the plagues that God inflicted on Egypt in the Exodus story, as God sought to free the Israelites. A plague of hail and fire draws from Exodus 9:13-35, especially verse 23.

With this plague one-third of the earth is burned up. There is an intensifying here. In the seals series, one-quarter of things are destroyed. Now it is one-third.

8:8-9

[8]The second angel blew his trumpet, and something like a great mountain, burning with fire, was thrown into the sea. [9]A third of the sea became blood, a third of the living creatures in the sea died, and a third of the ships were destroyed.

The second angel blows the trumpet and something like a great mountain, burning with fire, is thrown into the sea. One-third of the sea becomes like blood. Again this recalls the plagues against Egypt, Exodus 7:17.

8:10-11

[10]The third angel blew his trumpet, and a great star fell from heaven, blazing like a torch, and it fell on a third of the rivers and on the springs of water. [11]The name of the star is Wormwood. A third of the waters became wormwood, and many died from the water, because it was made bitter.

The next angel blows his trumpet and a great star falls from heaven. It is blazing like a torch and falls on one-third of the waters. The star is named "Wormwood," which is a shrub with a very bitter taste.[1] The water is made bitter and people die from drinking it. This plague does not draw from the plagues against Egypt. It is instead drawn from Jeremiah 23:15, an Old Testament word of judgment.

8:12

[12]The fourth angel blew his trumpet, and a third of the sun was struck, and a third of the moon, and a third of the stars, so that a third of their light was darkened; a third of the day was kept from shining, and likewise the night.

The fourth angel blows the trumpet and a third of the sun and moon and stars are struck. There is darkness. This again recalls the plagues against Egypt (Exod 10:21-29).

---

[1] Leonard Thompson, *Revelation*, Abingdon New Testament Commentaries (Nashville: Abingdon Press, 1998), 116.

8:13

¹³Then I looked, and I heard an eagle crying with a loud voice as it flew in midheaven, "Woe, woe, woe to the inhabitants of the earth, at the blasts of the other trumpets that the three angels are about to blow!"

As if all this isn't enough, an eagle now flies in mid-heaven and announces, woe to the inhabitants of the earth at the blowing of the next three trumpets. "The inhabitants of the earth" is one of John's ways of referring to those who do not follow God. These inhabitants are warned that things are about to get even worse!

Judgment

What do we do with all this? These are threats of judgment, harsh judgment. The threats make us uneasy. How are we to understand this? Three things are important to keep in mind:

1. John is drawing heavily in this chapter (and in the entire book) from the Old Testament Exodus story. In the Exodus story, God sent plagues as part of his judgment on the sins of the Egyptians. But remember that the plagues served the goal of the redemption of God's people. The point of the plagues was to set the people of Israel free; the judgment led to redemption. That is also the case here. God will judge a sinful world, but the judgment serves the cause of redemption. God will judge and destroy evil in order that he might make his world new and whole. God's ultimate goal is the redemption of his creation.

2. These words of judgment also function as warning. It is helpful here to go back to chapters 2 and 3. One of the temptations facing the seven churches was to accommodate to the ways of the world. The Nicolaitans and Balaam and Jezebel could argue that it wasn't that big of a thing to accommodate to Roman ways. John in chapters 8 and 9 is pointing out, it is that big of a thing. The judgments of chapters 8 and 9 show how God is going to deal with the ways of the world. Christians must not accommodate themselves to that which is going to be judged. What John is doing is using stark language, language of warning, to tell the Christians not to accommodate themselves to the ways of a sinful world.

3. Perhaps the question we as modern readers need to ask is, will God also judge some of the things in our modern culture to which we have accommodated ourselves? For example, twenty-first century Americans live in a materialistic culture, a culture that strays from the biblical

teachings of giving and stewardship and justice. Yet most of us have managed to accommodate ourselves to materialistic ways. Twenty-first century Americans live in a culture that has become comfortable with much drug and alcohol use and abuse. Again we accommodate to the ways of the world. One of the functions of the words of judgment in Revelation is to wake us up to the challenges and evils of our day. We, like first-century Christians in Asia Minor, need to learn to stand against that which is not pleasing to our God.

Chapter 9

9:1-12

And the fifth angel blew his trumpet, and I saw a star that had fallen from heaven to earth, and he was given the key to the shaft of the bottomless pit; [2]he opened the shaft of the bottomless pit, and from the shaft rose smoke like the smoke of a great furnace, and the sun and the air were darkened with the smoke from the shaft. [3]Then from the smoke came locusts on the earth, and they were given authority like the authority of scorpions of the earth. [4]They were told not to damage the grass of the earth or any green growth or any tree, but only those people who do not have the seal of God on their foreheads. [5]They were allowed to torture them for five months, but not to kill them, and their torture was like the torture of a scorpion when it stings someone. [6]And in those days people will see death but will not find it; they will long to die, but death will flee from them.

[7]In appearance the locusts were like horses equipped for battle. On their heads were what looked like crowns of gold; their faces were like human faces, [8]their hair like women's hair, and their teeth like lions' teeth; [9]they had scales like iron breastplates, and the noise of their wings was like the noise of many chariots with horses rushing into battle. [10]They have tails like scorpions, with stingers, and in their tails is their power to harm people for five months. [11]They have as king over them the angel of the bottomless pit; his name in Hebrew is Abaddon, and in Greek he is called Apollyon.

[12]The first woe has passed. There are still two woes to come.

The fifth angel blows his trumpet and a star falls from heaven to earth. In Jewish thought this falling star would be understood as an angel. This angel opens the bottomless pit. Again in Jewish thought, there was the idea of a bottomless pit as a place of banishment for angels that had revolted against God.[2] As the angel opens the pit, smoke comes

---

[2] Adela Yarbro Collins, *The Apocalypse New Testament Message* 22 (Collegeville, MN: Liturgical Press, 1979), 60.

out, followed by locust. These locusts do not damage plants, but humans. They torture those who are not sealed by God.

The fifth and sixth trumpets take on a surreal quality. John is intentionally creating a nightmare. He uses imagery so bizarre that it overwhelms our imaginations. As if things weren't bad enough with the first four trumpets, John now pushes things to a new and horrifying level.

The fifth trumpet continues the tie-in with the story of the plagues of the Exodus. A plague of locusts was the eighth plague on Egypt (Exodus 10). The repeated reference to five months is a reference to the life span of a locust. The locusts here are given a bizarre description. They wear crowns of gold and have a human face (evil often has a human face!). They have women's hair, teeth like a lion, iron breastplates. The description is chaotic, unreal. Perhaps John wants us to notice the contrast between God's ordered heavenly throne room with its living creatures in chapters 4 and 5, and the grotesque picture of evil here.[3]

The king of the bottomless pit is called in Greek Apollyon, which means destroyer. There is probably a bit of political satire here as John takes a shot at the Roman Emperor.[4] The emperor was a man named Domitian who liked to consider himself a descendant of the god Apollo. John here paints a most unflattering reference, comparing the emperor and his followers to grasshoppers!

Once again John's intent with this imagery is to overwhelm us. The descriptions are so nightmarish, so bizarre, that they create a feeling of evil and revulsion. One of the things that John is doing is announcing judgment on the pagan world in such ghastly terms that Christians will know not to accommodate themselves to it.

John's imagery here cannot be fit into our normal terms of space and time. For example, the geography here is clearly symbolic. We can't ask where on a map the opening to the bottomless pit is. Likewise, we have already pointed out that Revelation cannot be put onto a neat timeline, as if we wanted to use it to draw a map to the future. That is again the case here. This imagery is so bizarre, we can't fit it on a time line. As we deal with this material, the best approach is to ask what John is trying to do with this imagery. What John is doing is announcing judgment in such horrible terms that Christians will instinctively recoil against it.

[3] Craig Koester, *Revelation and the End of All Things,* (Wm. Eerdmans Publishing Company, 2001), 100.
[4] G. B. Caird, *A Commentary on the Revelation of Saint John the Divine* (New York: Harper & Row, 1966), 120.

9:13-19

[13]Then the sixth angel blew his trumpet, and I heard a voice from the four horns of the golden altar before God, [14]saying to the sixth angel who had the trumpet, "Release the four angels who are bound at the great river Euphrates." [15]So the four angels were released, who had been held ready for the hour, the day, the month, and the year, to kill a third of humankind. [16]The number of the troops of cavalry was two hundred million; I heard their number. [17]And this was how I saw the horses in my vision: the riders wore breastplates the color of fire and of sapphire and of sulfur; the heads of the horses were like lions' heads, and fire and smoke and sulfur came out of their mouths. [18]By these three plagues a third of humankind was killed, by the fire and smoke and sulfur coming out of their mouths. [19]For the power of the horses is in their mouths and in their tails; their tails are like serpents, having heads; and with them they inflict harm.

The sixth trumpet is blown and four angels who were bound at the great river Euphrates are released. In addition, a ghastly cavalry of 200 million now comes. This is an unbelievable number. Even in our modern day, we can't move an army of 200 million. (In the 2003 war with Iraq, it took the United States a number of months to move 250,000 soldiers. This would be 800 times as many!) The cavalry is described in surreal, bizarre, and nightmarish terms, quite similar to the previous descriptions in chapter 9.

In John's description of the cavalry, there are unmistakable references to the Parthians. Remember, the Parthians were the empire to the east of the Roman Empire. The Romans could not subdue the Parthians and lived with a deep fear of them. John is playing with that fear. The border between the Parthians and the Romans was the Euphrates River. The reference to horses that sting with their heads and tails is a reference to the mounted bowmen of the Parthians. The Parthian cavalry had developed a technique of using mounted bowmen who could shoot both forwards and backwards as they overran enemy troops. The Romans couldn't figure out how to stop that. What John is doing is taking a contemporary fear, namely the Parthians, and raising it to a supernatural level. John is pounding away at the readers' imaginations with images of judgment. Once again his imagery is overwhelming, nightmarish.

9:20-21

[20]The rest of humankind, who were not killed by these plagues, did not repent of the works of their hands or give up worshipping demons and idols of gold and sliver and bronze and stone and wood, which cannot see or hear or walk. [21]And they did not repent of their murders or their sorceries or their fornication or their thefts.

With verses 20 and 21, we come to the punch line for chapters 8 and 9. The first six trumpets have been horrible. We recoil at the images; we begin to wonder how God could allow such things. The inevitable question of chapters 8 and 9 is, hasn't this been too much judgment? But now we learn that humankind still does not repent! All this horror, all this judgment, and it is not enough! People still will not listen to God. As incredible as it seems, people continue with their idolatry, their sins, and their evil.

These last verses of chapter 9 raise two important questions. First, just how hard is the human heart? We hear of all of this horrifying judgment, and then learn that people still refuse to repent. Are we human beings truly that hardened against God? As we finish chapter 9 we need to reflect on just how deep our alienation from God must be, if even all this judgment can't force us to deal with our Creator.

Then the second question, what is God to do? There have been the seven seals and the seven trumpets. Even with all that judgment, humankind still will not listen to God. How will God reach out to a sinful humanity? God has a plan and we will learn of it in chapters 10 and 11.

Section VI
God's Plan

Chapters 10–11

Judgment has not brought people back to God, but now in this section God announces a new plan. He will use the suffering of Christians to lead lost people back to himself. As God used the suffering of Jesus to redeem the world, so God will now use the suffering of Christians to lead people to himself.

Chapter 11 is perhaps the most difficult chapter of the book. The imagery is complicated and moving. But it is also a profound chapter, sharing an astonishing plan. God will use the faithful suffering of Christians to reach a rebellious humanity.

Chapter 10

> ## 10:1-3a
>
> And I saw another mighty angel coming down from heaven, wrapped in a cloud, with a rainbow over his head; his face was like the sun, and his legs like pillars of fire. ²He held a little scroll open in his hand. Setting his right foot on the sea and his left foot on the land, ³he gave a great shout, like a lion roaring.

Another mighty angel comes from heaven. John gives a quite detailed description of this angel. It is a description of power and grandeur, a description of rich symbolism and association. The angel is "wrapped in a cloud," which is a reminder of the divine presence. There is "a rainbow over his head," a reminder of divine mercy, of promise. His face "like the sun" recalls the description of Christ in 1:16. "Legs like pillars of fire" echoes Israel's journey in the wilderness where God led with a pillar of fire by day. The angel "held a little scroll open in his hand," much like God holds a scroll in chapter 5. Finally, the angel has a foot on land and sea. This echoes Daniel 12:5-13. (However, Daniel has three angels, one on each bank of a river and one above the river.) This angel's message will be for all the world!

We need also to focus on this "little scroll" in the hand of the angel. We should think of this scroll in terms of the scroll in God's hand in chapter 5. In chapter 5 the scroll in the hand of God is introduced by "a mighty angel" (v. 2). Now "another mighty angel" comes with a scroll in his hand. Some scholars have argued that this second scroll is actually the first scroll, only now having been opened by Jesus. This is a possible reading. However, G. B. Caird has an insight that is more persuasive. That is that the scrolls are certainly related.[1] The great scroll in chapter 5 contains the purpose of God to be achieved in Jesus. The little scroll of chapter 10 contains God's purpose for the church.[2] In fact, we will find in chapter 11 that the little scroll proclaims that as Christ conquered by suffering and dying, so now the church is called to do the same.

---

[1] G.B. Caird, *A Commentary on the Revelation of Saint John the Divine* (New York: Harper & Row, 1966), 126.

[2] Ibid.

10:3b-4

And when he shouted, the seven thunders sounded. ⁴And when the seven thunders had sounded, I was about to write, but I heard a voice from heaven saying, "Seal up what the seven thunders have said, and do not write it down."

When the angel speaks, seven thunders sound. We are not told what the thunders say. In fact John is instructed not to write down what the thunders say. Perhaps the thunders are another series of judgment, like the seals and the trumpets. If so, God is now withholding judgment as he begins a new plan. Whatever the thunders said, they serve to remind us that we do not have total access to the ways of heaven or to the mind of God. Our understanding is limited, and God does not reveal everything to us.

10:5-7

⁵Then the angel whom I saw standing on the sea and the land raised his right hand to heaven ⁶and swore by him who lives forever and ever, who created heaven and what is in it, the earth and what is in it, and the sea and what is in it: "There will be no more delay, ⁷but in the days when the seventh angel is to blow his trumpet, the mystery of God will be fulfilled, as he announced to his servants the prophets."

The angel raises his right hand to heaven and swears by God that there will be no more delay. Note how God is described in this verse, as the Creator of heaven and earth and sea and all that is in them. In the midst of judgment we are reminded that God's fundamental identity is Creator, not destroyer.[3] Moreover, the angel announces that there will be no more delay. John draws this imagery from Daniel 12:6-7, although in Daniel there is a delay before God acts. John now proclaims, no more delay. God will reveal a plan in chapter 11 that will begin immediately. (And in point of fact, the revealed plan has begun and does continue even in our day!)

The angel further announces that the "mystery of God will be fulfilled." The mystery is not about God's saving purpose. The Christians already knew that God's purpose is to save. The mystery is how God will achieve this purpose.[4] This will be revealed in chapter 11.

---

[3] Craig Koester, *Revelation and the End of All Things* (Grand Rapids: Wm. Eerdmans Publishing Company, 2001), 103.

[4] Ibid.

10:8-11

[8]Then the voice that I had heard from heaven spoke to me again, saying, "Go, take the scroll that is open in the hand of the angel who is standing on the sea and on the land." [9]So I went to the angel and told him to give me the little scroll; and he said to me, "Take it, and eat; it will be bitter to your stomach, but sweet as honey in your mouth." [10]So I took the little scroll from the hand of the angel and ate it; it was sweet as honey in my mouth, but when I had eaten it, my stomach was made bitter. [11]Then they said to me, "You must prophesy again about many peoples and nations and languages and kings."

John is instructed to take the scroll from the angel and eat it. This draws on imagery from Ezekiel 3:1-2, where the prophet Ezekiel is instructed to eat a scroll. What a great image this is for internalizing the Word of God! We don't just study the Word at a distance. We are to internalize the Word and make it part of our very being!

The scroll is sweet in John's mouth but bitter to his stomach. There will be a sweetness to the message, as it will involve the salvation of the nations. But there is bitterness too, as it will involve the suffering and death of Christians. As Caird points out, "the way of victory is the way of the Cross."[5]

The point of these verses is that John is re-commissioned as a prophet. He is given a message to speak to "many peoples and nations." Chapter 10 has set the stage for chapter 11. In chapter 11 we learn what this new revelation is.

Chapter 11

11:1-2

Then I was given a measuring rod like a staff, and I was told, "Come and measure the temple of God and the altar and those who worship there, [2]but do not measure the court outside the temple; leave that out, for it is given over to the nations, and they will trample over the holy city for forty-two months."

Chapter 11 begins with John being instructed to measure the temple. This idea of measuring is drawn from Ezekiel, who had a vision of an

---

[5] Caird, 130.

angel measuring the temple, and Zechariah, who had a vision of an angel measuring Jerusalem. John adapts these Old Testament visions to his message.

An important question to ask of this passage is what does John mean by the temple? Some commentators on Revelation insist that the temple refers to the physical temple in Jerusalem. There are problems with this, however. First, there was no physical temple when John wrote. The Romans had destroyed the temple in Jerusalem in 70 A.D., about 25 years before the writing of Revelation. Second, if John is interested in a physical building, it is surprising that he gives us no details or dimensions of the building. Third, John simply does not operate that literally in the book. For John to shift from being quite symbolic in his writing to now being quite literal is highly doubtful.

A better interpretation, more consistent with Revelation's style, is to read temple symbolically and see it as the people of God or the Christian community. Besides fitting in with John's style, there are two other arguments to support this reading. First, this interpretation ties in with John's imagery in 3:12, where Christians are promised they will be built into the temple. The temple is the community of believers. Second, this usage fits in well with the rest of the New Testament. In the New Testament as a whole, the temple is often used as a way of talking about the Christian community (for example, see 1 Cor 3:16, Eph 2:20, 1 Pet 2:5). We do well to understand the temple as symbolizing the Christian community.

Given this, what does it mean to measure the temple? Measuring the temple refers to the preservation of the Christian community, and particularly the preservation of true service to God within the community.[6] The measuring is God's promise of care for his people, even in the face of trials and persecutions to come.

John next adds a reference to 42 months. We will see this reference repeatedly in the rest of Revelation, either as 42 months or 1260 days or three and a half years. This is a reference to a time of persecution. In the Old Testament book of Daniel, the Jewish people faced a 42-month struggle with a ruler named Antiochus Epiphanies. The struggle included the desecration of the temple in Jerusalem, much persecution, and was a horribly difficult time for the Jews. The memory of this struggle was well burned into the Jewish mind of John's time. A reference to 42 months (or its equivalent) would be quickly understood as a reference

---

[6] Koester, 106. For a fuller treatment of what it means to measure the temple, please see Koester, p. 104–108.

to a period of persecution. We do well to recognize this language, not as a prediction of an exact period of time, but as a reference to a coming time of persecution and challenge.

Given all this, the measuring of the temple in verses 1 and 2 is a promise of God's care for his people even in the time of upcoming persecution. John foresees persecutions to come, but he wants to assure the Christians of God's care for them. Note how the inner sanctuary is measured and kept safe, which refers to the preservation of true worship and service of God, even during the persecution. The outer court is not measured, which refers to part of the Christian community coming under the sway of the pagan world.[7] As John has pointed out in chapters 2 and 3, this was a real temptation and struggle for the seven churches, and was beginning already.

11:3-6

[3]"And I will grant my two witnesses authority to prophesy for one thousand two hundred sixty days, wearing sackcloth."

[4]These are the two olive trees and the two lampstands that stand before the Lord of the earth. [5]And if anyone wants to harm them, fire pours from their mouth and consumes their foes; anyone who wants to harm them must be killed in this manner. [6]They have authority to shut the sky, so that no rain may fall during the days of their prophesying, and they have authority over the waters to turn them into blood, and to strike the earth with every kind of plague, as often as they desire.

Two witnesses are now granted to prophesy. These witnesses are described as "the two olive trees and the two lampstands." Who are they? The two witnesses represent "the church in its faithful witness to the world."[8] This is the church, Christians, called to witness to Jesus. John uses deliberate language to make this point. The image of two lampstands is drawn from chapter 1, where John has already told us that the lampstands refer to the churches (1:20). The two olive trees recall Zechariah 3:14, where two olive trees refer to the anointed king and priest. In John's imagery, this kingly and priestly imagery again refers to the church.[9] Moreover, there are two witnesses because in Deuteronomic law (Deut 19:15), two witnesses are required to bear witness to the truth.

[7] Ibid., 107.
[8] Richard Bauckham, *The Theology of the Book of Revelation,* New Testament Theology, (Cambridge: University Press, 1993), 84.
[9] Caird, 134.

The two witnesses are the church, which is called to bear witness to Jesus. The 42 months or 1260 days is a reminder that the church is called to bear faithful witness even in a period of persecution and tribulation. The message which the witnesses/church share is one of repentance. This is indicated by the witnesses being clothed in sackcloth, an Old Testament sign of repentance. The church is to live in a posture of repentance and call the world to repentance.

The witnesses/church work with incredible power. John draws on Old Testament references to Moses and Elijah to say that the church speaks and works in the power of God. (Perhaps we in the church underestimate the power we have in the Risen Lord!)

11:7-10

[7]When they have finished their testimony, the beast that comes up from the bottomless pit will make war on them and conquer them and kill them, [8]and their dead bodies will lie in the street of the great city that is prophetically called Sodom and Egypt, where also their Lord was crucified. [9]For three and a half days members of the peoples and tribes and languages and nations will gaze at their dead bodies and refuse to let them be placed in a tomb; [10]and the inhabitants of the earth will gloat over them and celebrate and exchange presents, because these two prophets had been a torment to the inhabitants of the earth.

After the witnesses finish their testimony, the beast comes up from the bottomless pit to make war on them and to kill them. This is the first reference in Revelation to the beast. We will hear much more of the beast in the chapters to follow. For now we need to note that the beast is a reference to the Roman Empire. The beast kills the witnesses.

The witnesses lie dead in the street for three and a half days. The great city in which they lie is identified as Sodom, Egypt, and the place where Jesus was crucified, Jerusalem. We certainly cannot take this reference literally, as these are three very different locations! We do better to think not of a specific city or event, but of what happens to Christian martyrs again and again, in many times and places.

The bodies are not buried. This is a sign of deep disrespect. The inhabitants of the earth gloat over the dead witnesses, and even exchange presents. The world is not eager to hear the teachings of God!

11:11-13

[11]But after the three and a half days, the breath of life from God entered them, and they stood on their feet, and those who saw them were terrified. [12]Then they heard a loud voice from heaven saying to them, "Come up here!" And they went up to heaven in a cloud while their enemies watched them. [13]At that moment there was a great earthquake, and a tenth of the city fell; seven thousand people were killed in the earthquake, and the rest were terrified and gave glory to the God of heaven.

After three and a half days, the breath of God enters the bodies, and they return to life. (This recalls Ezekiel 37.) The witnesses are raised to heaven. The people who see this are terrified. There follows a great earthquake, and seven thousand people die. *But the rest of the people give glory to God. There is repentance. Now, finally, there is repentance, and nine-tenths of the inhabitants turn to God!*

What are we to do with this story? Let me share an interpretation.[10] The question at the end of chapter 9 is, how is God going to reach a world that will not listen to him? Judgment has not succeeded. Here in chapter 11 we are given God's plan. God will use the church. Christians will witness to Jesus, and they will be killed for that. But God will use their deaths to reach out to the world. As the inhabitants of the world see how Christians are able to face death in the promise of the resurrection, the inhabitants will see the reality of the resurrection. Will the inhabitants of the earth literally see the Christians raised? No. But as they see the Christians being faithful unto death, they will see a clear witness to the resurrection.

As a pastor, I've seen this happen. I've watched in hospital rooms as people have died, but done so in such a faithful manner that the family and medical staff all leave the room knowing they've caught a glimpse of heaven. In the faithful witness of Christians, we catch a view of the heaven to come!

As the inhabitants of the earth see the Christians' faithful witness, the inhabitants will come to God. Not all, of course. But nine-tenths will.

What is God's plan to redeem the world? As the inhabitants of the world see the faithful witness of Christians, even unto death, they will repent. Judgment has not brought repentance, but this will! God will use the self-sacrifice of Christians to lead the world back to faith. Note

---

[10] In this interpretation I am drawing heavily from Richard Bauckham in his book *The Theology of the Book of Revelation,* especially pages 84–88.

the severe call to discipleship here. Christians are called, like Jesus, to give of themselves, even their lives, for the sake of the world. (Remember in chapter 10 that this message is sweet and bitter!) This is the way of the cross.

We also know from history that this plan has worked. We know from church history that the persecutions did come and the Christians did die. In the years following Revelation, many Christians did die for the faith. As nonbelievers saw that, and particularly saw how faithfully the Christians died, the nonbelievers were converted. In fact, finally even the Roman Empire was converted. The faithful suffering and death of Christians did lead many to faith. (An early church leader, Tertullian, said, "The blood of the martyrs is the seed of the church.") Remember back in chapter 10 the angel said no more delay. This plan has begun and it has worked!

Moreover, this is still God's plan. In many places of the world today, Christians still suffer and die for the faith. Incredibly, in these places the church is growing by leaps and bounds. God's plan is still working. As Christians dare to be faithful even unto death, people are led back to God.

We as modern Christians do well to think through what this means for our life of faith. We are called to give of ourselves for the sake of the world. In our giving and sacrifice, the world sees the truth of Jesus. This is the way of the cross and the way of salvation.

11:14

The second woe has passed. The third woe is coming very soon.

John now in an almost editorial comment tells us that the second woe has passed. He also points out that the third woe is yet to come. What is odd about this is that the third woe is not highlighted in the rest of the book. Scholars have wondered what the third woe is, and what happened to it. The best interpretation is that the third woe refers to "destroying those who destroy the earth" in 11:18, the final destruction of evil as God's kingdom comes.[11]

---

[11] Adela Yarbro Collins, *The Apocalypse New Testament Message 22* (Collegeville, MN: Liturgical Press, 1979), 74.

11:15-19

[15]Then the seventh angel blew his trumpet, and there were loud voices in heaven, saying, "The kingdom of the world has become the kingdom of our Lord and of his Messiah, and he will reign forever and ever." [16]Then the twenty-four elders who sit on their thrones before God fell on their faces and worshiped God, [17]singing, "We give you thanks, Lord God Almighty, who are and who were, for you have taken your great power and begun to reign. [18]The nations raged, but your wrath has come, and the time for judging the dead, for rewarding your servants, the prophets and saints and all who fear your name, both small and great, and for destroying those who destroy the earth."

[19]Then God's temple in heaven was opened, and the ark of his covenant was seen within his temple; and there were flashes of lightning, rumblings, peals of thunder, an earthquake, and heavy hail.

Finally the seventh angel blows his trumpet. Now the end comes! The kingdom of God comes amidst songs of triumph and praise. "The kingdom of the world has become the kingdom of our Lord—He has begun to reign!" The victory and the kingdom are here. Note in verse 16 God is described as "who are and who were." There is no more reference to "who is to come," because that has now been accomplished. The kingdom is here.

Verse 19 speaks of God's temple in heaven being opened, and the ark of the covenant being revealed there. This is a reference to Jewish expectation. The expectation was that when the kingdom of God comes, the Old Testament ark of the covenant would be revealed in heaven. Once again the message is that the kingdom has come!

We could expect the book of Revelation to end here. The earth has been judged, God's plan has brought people to faith, the kingdom has come. What is left to happen? But of course the book does not end here. John has much more to tell us. He will "take us through the cycle" again. He will also further develop and deepen the themes he has introduced in the first eleven chapters.

Section VII

Evil Exposed

Chapters 12–13

Some scholars break Revelation into an "Act I and Act II" format. In a sense with the end of chapter 11, we have reached the end of Act I. There is a natural break here. We take a breath, then start again as we move into chapter 12.

In chapters 12 and 13 John uses picturesque and even mythological language. He begins in chapter 12 by adapting a Roman myth to portray Satan as a dragon waiting to consume God's people. Then, in chapter 13, John portrays the Roman Empire as a beast. Rome is "unmasked," revealing it not as a benevolent ruler but as an evil beast that receives its power from Satan the dragon. A good question to ask while reading these chapters is, are there evils in our world that need to be unmasked, evils that we too often accept but which need to be revealed as contrary to the will of God?

Chapter 12

> **12:1-6**
>
> A great portent appeared in heaven: a woman clothed with the sun, with the moon under her feet, and on her head a crown of twelve stars. [2]She was pregnant and was crying out in birthpangs, in the agony of giving birth. [3]Then another portent appeared in heaven: a great red dragon, with seven heads and ten horns, and seven diadems on his heads. [4]His tail swept down a third of the stars of heaven and threw them to the earth. Then the dragon stood before the woman who was about to bear a child, so that he might devour her child as soon as it was born. [5]And she gave birth to a son, a male child, who is to rule all the nations with a rod of iron. But her child was snatched away and taken to God and to his throne; [6]and the woman fled into the wilderness, where she has a place prepared by God, so that there she can be nourished for one thousand two hundred sixty days.

John works in chapter 12 with an ancient myth, a myth which he claims and reworks to proclaim a Christian message. There was an ancient Greek myth in which the dragon Python attempted to kill the newborn son of the god Zeus. The mother, Leto, fled to the island of Delos. There a son, Apollo, is born. Apollo goes on to kill the dragon. This myth and its variations were quite familiar in the ancient world.

The Romans had claimed and reworked this myth for their purposes. In Roman usage, the mother was identified as Roma, the goddess of Rome. The son was the Roman Emperor. (Remember that Domitian, the emperor at the time of the writing of Revelation, claimed to be a descendant of Apollo.) What the myth then proclaimed was that it was the Roman Emperor who subdued evil and established a great period of peace and prosperity.

John now claims this story and reworks it to proclaim his Christian message. John begins with the ancient myth, but weaves in his own imagery and rich Biblical imagery. The story becomes a Christian proclamation, with powerful symbolism and associations. In John's writing, the woman symbolizes the people of God. (This will become clearer as we move on in chapter 12.) The woman is described in glorious terms—clothed with the sun, the moon under her feet, a crown of twelve stars. The dragon is Satan. (John tells us that in verse 9.) Seven heads are a reminder of some of the seven-headed figures of evil in the Old Testament.

The seven diadems speak of Satan seeking and claiming power. The dragon is seeking the power that is meant for God alone. The child is Christ. When John writes that "the child is to rule all the nations with a rod of iron," that is a reference to Psalm 2, a psalm understood in Jewish thought as a prediction of the Messiah. In numerous places in Revelation John uses the image of "ruling with a rod of iron" to refer to Jesus.

In John's version of the story, Jesus is born of the people of God. Satan sought to stop Jesus, but Satan failed. Notice how John moves immediately from Jesus' birth to his enthronement in heaven. John doesn't here give any of the details of Jesus' life or ministry. He simply tells us that Satan attempted to stop Jesus. Satan failed, and now Jesus is enthroned in heaven. With Jesus' enthronement, the woman, the people of God, flee into the wilderness for 1260 days. Remember that this is a symbol for a period of persecution. The people of God flee into the wilderness in the face of persecution to come.[1]

12:7-12

[7]And war broke out in heaven; Michael and his angels fought against the dragon. The dragon and his angels fought back, [8]but they were defeated, and there was no longer any place for them in heaven. [9]The great dragon was thrown down, that ancient serpent, who is called the Devil and Satan, the deceiver of the whole world—he was thrown down to the earth, and his angels were thrown down with him.

[10]Then I heard a loud voice in heaven, proclaiming, "Now have come the salvation and the power and the kingdom of our God and the authority of his Messiah, for the accuser of our comrades has been thrown down, who accuses them day and night before our God. [11]But they have conquered him by the blood of the Lamb and by the word of their testimony, for they did not cling to life even in the face of death. [12]Rejoice then, you heavens and those who dwell in them! But woe to the earth and the sea, for the devil has come down to you with great wrath, because he knows that his time is short!"

War now breaks out in heaven. With the enthronement of Jesus, Michael and his angels begin an attack on this dragon Satan that has tried to overcome Jesus. Michael and his angels are victorious, and Satan is cast from heaven to the earth. Let's look in detail at some of the symbolism and messages in this account:

---

[1] In the Old Testament, the wilderness/desert is a place of mixed meaning. It is a place of trial and testing. It is also a place where God's people flee for safety and protection. This mixed meaning fits in beautifully with John's message in chapter 12.

In the Old Testament book of Daniel, Michael is identified as a prince or protector (Daniel 10 and 12). Michael in Daniel seems to be angelic or heavenly. Here he functions as a lead angel. Michael and the angels conquer "by the blood of the Lamb." John is clear that the cross of Jesus is the pivotal event in the victory over Satan. Further, in verse 10, Satan is stripped of his ability to accuse Christians before the throne of God, a reference to the Hebrew of the Old Testament, where "Satan" means "accuser." Verse 11 echoes the themes that have just been presented in chapter 11. The witness and death of Christians becomes an important part of God's plan.

This story proclaims that because of the victory of Jesus, Satan's sphere of activity is limited. Satan has been kicked out of heaven. But for the time being, he is still active on the earth. And the earth is warned! Satan, like a mad dog on a short leash, is out to do all the damage he can.

What John is doing here is proclaiming two basic tenets of Christian thought, but doing so in picturesque form. First, Jesus has won the victory in his death and resurrection. We can be confident of that. Satan is defeated, rejected. But second, until the Second Coming, Satan is still active here on the earth. He is out to wreak as much havoc as he can, and we need to be warned of that.

12:13-17

[13]So when the dragon saw that he had been thrown down to the earth, he pursued the woman who had given birth to the male child. [14]But the woman was given the two wings of the great eagle, so that she could fly from the serpent into the wilderness, to her place where she is nourished for a time, and times, and half a time. [15]Then from his mouth the serpent poured water like a river after the woman, to sweep her away with the flood. [16]But the earth came to the help of the woman; it opened its mouth and swallowed the river that the dragon had poured from his mouth. [17]Then the dragon was angry with the woman, and went off to make war on the rest of her children, those who keep the commandments of God and hold the testimony of Jesus.

The dragon Satan is thrown down to the earth and pursues the woman/people of God. He intends to make war on her. But the woman is given the wings of an eagle to escape into the wilderness. This reference to eagle's wings recalls Old Testament messages of deliverance by God. For example, "I bore you on eagles' wings and brought you to myself" (Exod 19:4) and "They shall mount up with wings like eagles"

(Isa 40:31). Just as in the Old Testament, God will lift up and care for his people.

The woman is taken to the wilderness for protection. She is nourished for "a time, and times, and half a time." Here again is a reference to a period of tribulation—three and a half times. Once again the point is made: God will nourish his people even in times of tribulation. The dragon/serpent continues the attack, pouring out water to sweep away the woman. But the very earth comes to rescue the woman. The story closes with the dragon being angry with the woman, and making war on her children, "those who keep the commandments of God and hold the testimony of Jesus."

In this section, Satan is continuing to attack Christians, and God is continually rescuing and caring for Christians. John is warning the early Christians (and us!) that Satan is and will be active. But the story, with all its Old Testament associations, is also a word of assurance that God will take care of his people. The God who has cared for his people throughout history will continue to care for his faithful ones.

What John is doing in Chapter 12 is using a common myth in the ancient world to help the Christians understand their situation. John warns the Christians that there is a battle going on, a battle between God and Satan. The Christians are told they are part of the battle, as Satan is out to get them. But the Christians are also assured of God's ultimate victory, and of God's ongoing care for them.

Chapter 12 is a symbolic, picturesque story that also warns and assures us. We are warned to live with eyes open, as Satan will attack God's people in a variety of ways. Perhaps we will be attacked with persecution, as was the case in Smyrna. Perhaps we will be lulled by complacency, the attack in Laodicea. We are warned that Satan will pursue God's people in every way he can. But we are also assured that the ultimate victory lies with the God who time and again has delivered his people.

Chapter 13

We will start chapter 13 with 12:18, because 12:18 fits in best with the verses that follow.

12:18–13:4

[18]Then the dragon took his stand on the sand of the seashore. [1]And I saw a beast rising out of the sea, having ten horns and seven heads; and on its horns were ten diadems, and on its heads were blasphemous names.

> ²And the beast that I saw was like a leopard, its feet were like a bear's, and its mouth was like a lion's mouth. And the dragon gave it his power and his throne and great authority. ³One of its heads seemed to have received a death-blow, but its mortal wound had been healed. In amazement the whole earth followed the beast. ⁴They worshipped the dragon, for he had given his authority to the beast, and they worshiped the beast, saying, "Who is like the beast, and who can fight against it?"

The dragon Satan now takes his stand on the seashore. While John's attention is directed to the sea, a beast rises out of it. In the description that follows, we discern that the beast is the Roman Empire. John describes the beast in picturesque language:

*The beast has "ten horns, seven heads, and ten diadems." The seven heads once again remind us of figures of evil in the Old Testament. The ten horns and the ten diadems tell us that this beast has power and claims power.

*On the heads of the beast are blasphemous names. John will develop this more in a few verses. For now we note that the Roman Emperors often were referred to as "lord and god."

*The beast is described as "like a leopard, its feet were like a bear's and its mouth was like a lion's mouth." This imagery comes from Daniel 7. In Daniel, four ancient empires are described in terms of a leopard, a bear, a lion, and as having ten horns. These ancient empires had challenged and persecuted Israel. John now draws on this imagery and says that Rome is a composite of all this ancient evil, an even greater evil than the evil of the Old Testament empires.

*The beast comes from the sea. There are two reasons for this. In the Old Testament the sea was a symbol of chaos and evil. It would be an appropriate beginning place for the beast. Second, in practical terms, the Romans came to Asia Minor by sea.

John next makes an incredible point. The dragon gives its power to the beast. In other words, Roman power comes from Satan! Roman authority, Roman power, and Roman grandeur are all rooted in Satan. John, in pointed and provocative language, is asking the Christians, do you really want to accommodate yourselves to this? What seemed like a minor issue back in chapters 2 and 3, namely accommodating Roman ways, is now revealed to be a compromise with Satan himself.

In verse 3 John goes on to write that one of the heads of the beast had received a death-blow, but the mortal wound was healed. This image functions in two ways. First, as is often the case in Revelation, evil parodies God. Jesus has risen from the dead; this evil beast has a mortal wound that is healed. Evil tries to look like something good. Second, John is making a reference here to the Nero legend. Nero was Roman emperor from 54–68 A.D. He was the first emperor to persecute Christians. (Nero had Christians covered in animal skins and thrown to dogs, he crucified Christians, and he burned them to death.) Nero committed suicide in 68 A.D. but there were strong rumors in the empire that Nero was either still alive or would return. (In fact, one of the rumors was that Nero would return to lead a Parthian army against Rome. We know from history that Nero imposters actually went to the Parthians and tricked them for a while.) A beast with a healed mortal wound would have reminded ancient readers of Nero. We do well to be careful here. John is not saying that the beast is to be equated with Nero. But he is saying that Nero was a good example of what the beast is about. The beast, namely the Roman Empire, will continue to do the things that Nero did.

John continues his description of the beast by pointing out that the whole earth followed the beast. That certainly was the case in the first century, when it seemed as if the whole world was following the Roman Empire and the ways of Rome. Moreover, as John points out, who can fight against this beast Rome? Roman might guaranteed that Rome would have its way.

13:5-10

[5]The beast was given a mouth uttering haughty and blasphemous words, and it was allowed to exercise authority for forty-two months. [6]It opened its mouth to utter blasphemies against God, blaspheming his name and his dwelling, that is, those who dwell in heaven. [7]Also it was allowed to make war on the saints and to conquer them. It was given authority over every tribe and people and language and nation, [8]and all the inhabitants of the earth will worship it, everyone whose name has not been written from the foundation of the world in the book of life of the Lamb that was slaughtered.

[9]Let anyone who has an ear listen: [10]If you are to be taken captive, into captivity you go; if you kill with the sword, with the sword you must be killed. Here is a call for the endurance and faith of the saints.

John continues his description of the beast by writing that the beast was given a mouth uttering haughty and blasphemous words, and that it blasphemed against God. This is a reference to emperor worship. The practice had developed of referring to Roman Emperors in divine terms, such as "lord and god." Normally emperors were declared to be "gods" by the Roman Senate only after their deaths, although there were instances where the emperors Nero and Domitian were addressed as gods during their lifetimes. To John's mind, the terms "lord" and "god" were to be reserved only for the one true God. The Roman Emperor (and any political authority for that matter) must not infringe on what is the domain of God alone.

Moreover, Rome saw itself as the center of the world. The haughtiness of the Roman Empire was that it saw itself as the point of orientation for the world, the very center and core. To John's mind that position must belong to God and only God. One of the sins of the Roman Empire was to claim for itself too high a status.[2]

John next points out that the beast Rome will persecute Christians. As we have previously mentioned, John foresaw a period of persecution coming. John picks up this theme again in verse 7 when he writes that the beast is allowed to make war on the saints and even conquer them. In fact verse 5 reinforces this when John notes that the beast has authority for forty-two months. As was pointed out in chapter 11, forty-two months is best understood not as an exact time reference, but as a reference to a coming period of persecution. As in previous chapters, John is warning the Christians.

John continues by noting the universal appeal of the beast. "All the inhabitants of the earth," and everyone not written in the Lamb's book of life, will follow the beast. That was the case, as all the world seemed to follow Rome. John concludes his description with a proverb based on Jeremiah 15:2. The proverb basically says that some will be taken into captivity, some will be killed by the beast. The beast is a threat. But knowing that, the Christians are called to endurance and faith.

This description of the beast in verses 1-10 is meant to give Christians insight into the Roman Empire, and into what Rome really is. The Roman Empire is not a grand and glorious deliverer. It is a hideous beast that blasphemes God and kills Christians. Christians must be on guard against the ways of Rome. We do well to remember the flow of the story here, beginning in Chapter 12. John started this section by telling us of the rebellion of Satan in heaven. John has now traced a path from Satan and his rebellion to the Roman Empire. What John is saying, in stark and

---

[2] It is important to note that Revelation is not anti-government. But when the government claims ultimate allegiance, then the government has gone too far and must be opposed.

picturesque language, is that the Roman Empire is rooted in the ways of Satan.[3]

13:11-18

[11]Then I saw another beast that rose out of the earth; it had two horns like a lamb and it spoke like a dragon. [12]It exercises all the authority of the first beast on its behalf, and it makes the earth and its inhabitants worship the first beast, whose mortal wound had been healed. [13]It performs great signs, even making fire come down from heaven to earth in the sight of all; [14]and by the signs that it is allowed to perform on behalf of the beast, it deceives the inhabitants of earth, telling them to make an image for the beast that had been wounded by the sword and yet lived; [15]and it was allowed to give breath to the image of the beast so that the image of the beast could even speak and cause those who would not worship the image of the beast to be killed. [16]Also it causes all, both small and great, both rich and poor, both free and slave, to be marked on the right hand or the forehead, [17]so that no one can buy or sell who does not have the mark, that is the name of the beast or the number of its name. [18]This calls for wisdom: let anyone with understanding calculate the number of the beast, for it is the number of a person. Its number is six hundred sixty-six.

John now sees a second beast, this one rising out of the earth. This beast is best understood as local officials who supported Rome.[4] We know from history that local officials did work with Rome and promoted Roman ways. We also know that the Romans often made use of existing political institutions in administrating their empire.[5] These local officials not only collaborated with Rome, but also supported and lifted up Roman ideology. In fact the practice of emperor worship in Asia came not from the Romans but from the local officials.

There are two reasons why this second beast is said to rise from the land. First, John is drawing from Old Testament imagery. In the Old Tes-

---

[3] It is helpful to compare and contrast John's view of Rome with other New Testament views of government, and Roman government in particular. John sees Rome as an instrument of Satan. But in 1 Peter 2:13-17, Christians are told to accept the authority of the government, and to even "Honor the emperor." Paul in Romans 13:1 writes that Christians are to "be subject to the governing authorities, for there is no authority except from God."

The New Testament provides a variety of insights into the relationship of Christians with the government, insights that reflect different contexts and differing circumstances. We do well to explore John's view in Revelation in light of the whole of the New Testament as we seek to come to terms with the role of government in our world.

[4] For a fuller explanation of this, please see G. B. Caird, *A Commentary on the Revelation of Saint John the Divine* (New York: Harper & Row, 1966), 171ff.

[5] Ibid., 171.

tament there were two monsters or beasts, Behemoth and Leviathan. One was understood to be from the sea, the other from the land. But second, this new beast comes from the land because it is indigenous. It is the local priests and officials who cooperated with Rome.

The work of this second beast is to support and bear witness to the first beast. In other words, these local officials would work with and glorify Rome. This would include worship of the emperor and lifting up of Roman ways and ideologies. The words and actions of this beast will be lies and deceptions that lift up the ways of Rome.

This second beast will be later described in Revelation as a "false prophet" (16:13, 19:20, 20:10). John here says that the second beast has "two horns like a lamb," but "it spoke like a dragon." This evil beast tries to disguise itself to look good (like the Lamb), but when it speaks it reveals itself to be of Satan. John develops here an evil threesome of dragon, beast, and false prophet, a "counterfeit" or "unholy" trinity.

Craig Koester makes a helpful point in explaining how to read this section of chapter 13.[6] Koester points out that we should read this as political satire. What John is doing in these verses is making fun of the whole political system. The local officials did their best to keep the local populace loyal to Rome. John accuses them of deception, of faking great signs, of making images of the beast, of making images talk. We know from history that this deception was done. John mocks the work of local officials and accuses them of working with "the hokum that one expects to find at a sideshow in a traveling circus."[7] John's point is that Christians must not be swayed by this foolishness and deception.

John continues in verses 16 and 17 by writing about the "mark" of the beast. John points out that followers of the beast are "marked on the right hand or the forehead." A few comments on this are in order. First, what John is doing here is once again saying that evil parodies good. We have been told in previous chapters that God "seals" his saints. Now the beast "marks" his followers. Just as the seal of God is not a visible seal, so we do well to understand the mark of the beast as not being a visible mark. It is, rather, a question of allegiance, to whom do you belong? Second, John is asking the Christians, whose side will you choose? Will you be marked by the beast, i.e., will you be on Satan's side? Or will you be sealed by God, i.e., will you be on God's side? To John's mind there

---

[6] Craig Koester, *Revelation and the End of All Things* (Grand Rapids: Wm. Eerdmans Publishing Company, 2001), 130–131.

[7] Ibid., 130.

can be no middle ground. The ancient Christians (and modern day Christians!) are called to make a choice.

John continues all this by pointing out that "no one can buy or sell without the mark of the beast." This is a reference to economic hardships for Christians. The Christians were already hurting in their economic standing, as they could not participate in trade guilds and civic functions. And perhaps there is a reference here to Roman coins. Roman coins bore images and inscriptions to the emperors and sometimes identified the emperors as "son of god" or "son of the deified." John might be saying that Christians cannot use such coins. To be faithful to Jesus will create economic problems for the Christians.

666

Chapter 13 ends with one of the best-known images from the book of Revelation. John tells us the number of the beast is 666. Christians have wondered for centuries just what this means. It should be noted that this passage has been used to create much mischief and havoc in the church. People throughout the years have labeled their opponents as 666, and thereby declared them evil. Various church leaders and world leaders have been labeled as 666. (Ronald Wilson Reagan was even labeled as 666 by some fringe groups because he had six letters in each of his names.) This is an image that has been often twisted and misused.

We do well to note a number of things about this image. The first is that John likes symbols that can function at more than one level, and that is the case here. At one level, 666 is just short of 777. Seven is a number of completeness for the book of Revelation. 777 would be a number of perfection, of completeness. Six in Revelation functions as a number of incompleteness, of that which falls short. 666 is a number of imperfection, as it falls short of 777. John is labeling the beast Rome as imperfect and even as destructive.

There is a second level to this image. John is also dealing with the practice of gematria. In the ancient world, letters also functioned as numbers. "A" would be 1, "B" would be 2, etc. Given that, each name would also be a number. For example "Ada" would be 6 (a or 1, plus d or 4, plus a or 1 equals 6). When John invites us to "calculate the number of the beast," he is referring to the practice of gematria. (We should further note that in gematria, it is easy to work from the name to the number. It is much more difficult to work from the number back to the name!)

666 most likely stands for Nero. *Neron Kaiser*, the Hebrew form of Nero Caesar, in Hebrew characters adds up to 666.[8] Moreover, this would fit the context of chapter 13. John is not introducing a new argument at this point. He is summing up his prior arguments. He is drawing on imagery he has already used, namely the Nero legend, to finish up this section.[9]

What John is doing with the use of 666 is telling Christians once again to be careful with the ways of Rome. John is telling the Christians that in the final analysis, Rome looks an awful lot like Nero. The Roman Empire is finally a beast, a beast that bears a striking resemblance to the craziness and sin of Nero. The Christians must not accept or compromise with the ways of Rome.

A final question

We do well to end this study of chapter 13 with the question, what does the beast look like in our day? In Revelation, John pointed out to the Christians in first century Asia Minor that the Roman Empire was really a beast, rooted in the power of Satan. Part of John's purpose in writing Revelation was to "unmask" Rome so that Christians could see its true nature.

A good question to conclude chapter 13 is, are there beasts in our world that need to be unmasked and named as evil? As twenty-first century Christians, we know that Satan is still active. We have to believe that Satan is still empowering "beasts" in our day to do his will. The Roman Empire is long gone, but what in our day functions as a beast? Would the beast in our day look like evil governments in the world, or our materialism and consumerism, or perhaps our media fixation on violence and sex? The church is continually called to unmask that which is opposed to the will of God. As Adela Yarbro Collins so powerfully put it, the church of every age must name the beast.[10]

---

[8] In Hebrew letters Neron Kaiser is *nron qsr*. To put this in numbers, num (50) plus resh (200) plus waw (6) plus nun (50) plus qof (100) plus samech (60) plus resh (200) equals 666. For a fuller explanation of this, see Craig Koester's book *Revelation and the End of the Ages*, pages 132–134.

[9] Another advantage of this interpretation is that it allows us to understand a well-known variant on this passage. Some ancient copies of Revelation have 616 in place of 666. The Hebrew characters in *Nero Kaisar* add up to 616, and would explain the variant.

[10] Adela Yarbro Collins, *Crisis and Catharsis: The Power of the Apocalypse* (Philadelphia: Westminster, 1984), 175.

Section VIII

Pick a Side

Chapter 14

This section challenges Christians to pick a side. On one side John sets the ways of the world: the dragon, the beast, and the false prophet. On the other side is God's army: the Lamb and his followers. John says you cannot make your peace with both. Christians need to pick a side. It is a stark challenge for first century Christians and for twenty-first century Christians.

Chapter 14

14:1-5

Then I looked, and there was the Lamb, standing on Mount Zion! And with him were one hundred forty-four thousand who had his name and his Father's name written on their foreheads. ²And I heard a voice from heaven like the sound of many waters and like the sound of loud thunder; the voice I heard was like the sound of harpists playing on their harps, ³and they sing a new song before the throne and before the four living creatures and before the elders. No one could learn that song except the one hundred forty-four thousand who have been redeemed from the earth. ⁴It is these who have not defiled themselves with women, for they are virgins; these follow the Lamb wherever he goes. They have been redeemed from humankind as first fruits for God and the Lamb, ⁵and in their mouth no lie was found; they are blameless.

John shifts his focus from the evils on the earth to the glories of heaven above. He sees the Lamb and 144,000 people gathered on Mount Zion. Mount Zion is traditionally the place on which the temple was built in Jerusalem. It was understood in scripture as a place of safety and deliverance and worship. Here the reference is to a heavenly gathering place, as God gathers his redeemed in safety and victory.

On this heavenly Mount Zion is the Lamb, and the Lamb is joined by 144,000 people. These people have God and the Lamb's name on their foreheads. (This is reminiscent of 3:12, where those who conquer are promised God and the Lamb's name on their foreheads.) These 144,000 sing a new song before the throne of God, a song that only they know. Who are these 144,000? They are identified as "first fruits for God and the Lamb," the first of the redeemed, perhaps the martyrs. It also seems the case that, following John's imagery in 7:4, these people also represent the entire people of God. These are the ones who have conquered, who now share in the victory and glory of God.

John points out in verse 4 that these people are virgins. This is a problematic verse. Don't take this literally, as if John were making some sort of anti-sexuality statement. The 144,000 are better understood as an army, the army of God. In the Old Testament, soldiers were expected to refrain from sex before battles. These people are God's army who have fought a holy war, and therefore identified as having refrained from sex.

Moreover, John has frequently referred to idolatry as fornication and adultery. Now conversely he refers to these faithful ones as virgins.

Notice the contrast that John is setting up in chapters 13 and 14. On the one side are the dragon, the beast, and the false prophet. On the other side are the Lamb and his followers. What John is not so subtly saying is, "Pick a side!" John lays out two very distinct options, and tells his readers to pick one side or the other. The Christians in first century Asia Minor were tempted to try to accommodate their faith to Roman ways. John here is setting up a stark contrast to tell the Christians that they have to be on one side or the other. No compromise is possible. We as modern readers do well to see that John's words also raise the same challenge for us. We modern day Christians are often tempted to compromise our Christianity with the ways of our culture. John challenges us to pick one side or the other. To be faithful to Jesus means putting Jesus first, no matter what.

14:6-13

⁶Then I saw another angel flying in midheaven, with an eternal gospel to proclaim to those who live on the earth—to every nation and tribe and language and people. ⁷He said in a loud voice, "Fear God and give him glory, for the hour of his judgment has come; and worship him who made heaven and earth, the sea and the springs of water."

⁸Then another angel, a second, followed, saying, "Fallen, fallen is Babylon the great! She has made all nations drink of the wine of the wrath of her fornication."

⁹Then another angel, a third, followed them, crying with a loud voice, "Those who worship the beast and its image, and receive a mark on their foreheads or on their hands, ¹⁰they will also drink the wine of God's wrath, poured unmixed into the cup of his anger, and they will be tormented with fire and sulfur in the presence of the holy angels and in the presence of the Lamb. ¹¹And the smoke of their torment goes up forever and ever. There is no rest day or night for those who worship the beast and its image and for anyone who receives the mark of its name."

¹²Here is a call for the endurance of the saints, those who keep the commandments of God and hold fast to the faith of Jesus.

¹³And I heard a voice from heaven saying, "Write this: Blessed are the dead who from now on die in the Lord." "Yes," says the Spirit, "they will rest from their labors, for their deeds follow them."

Three angels now appear in midheaven. These angels reinforce the message of "Pick a side." The first angel begins by proclaiming, "Fear

God and give him glory." The message of this angel is to pick God's side, to worship God, and not to pick the side of Rome/Satan. A couple of comments are helpful on this first angel. The first angel is said to arrive with "an eternal gospel to proclaim to those who live on the earth—to every nation and tribe and language and people." "Gospel" means "good news." The Good News is the offer of redemption and new life in God and it is meant for all people. We do well to hear again that God's deepest desire in the book of Revelation is to lead all people to redemption. Revelation is never just a book of judgment. Time and again the point is made that God's desire is to lead all people to new life! Note also how God is described in verse 7. God is described in terms of his creating. We are once again reminded that God is ultimately creator and not destroyer. We are encouraged to pick God's side, the side of our Creator.

A second angel appears in verse 8. This angel announces that Babylon is fallen. This is the first mention in the book of Babylon. We will learn later in the book that Babylon refers to Rome. This message of destruction echoes Old Testament passages from Isaiah and Jeremiah. The message is that Rome will fall. Once again the call here is to pick a side. John is asking the Christians, do you really want to side with Rome, knowing that it will be destroyed?

A third angel appears in verse 9 and raises the ante even higher. This angel announces that those who accommodate themselves to Rome will face eternal punishment. The language here is extremely harsh; it is language of fire and smoke and torment. The message is stark and clear—do not accommodate yourselves to worldly ways and the judgment that will bring. Rather, be sure to pick God's side.

Many readers of Revelation find these words of the third angel to be overly harsh. They certainly are words of threat, words that make us uneasy. It is best to understand these words as words of warning. John is using the strongest language he can find to warn people from accommodating themselves to Rome. John uses harsh language to make a stark and unmistakable point—be sure to pick God's side.

John ends this section by reinforcing the message once again. He calls for "the endurance of the saints" (v. 12) and promises a blessing for those who die in the Lord (v. 13). We are once again directed to God and God alone.

Reflection

Let's stop for a bit and reflect on what John is doing here. In chapters 13 and 14 John is drawing two contrasting sides. On one side are the dragon Satan, the beast Rome, and the false prophet. On the other side are the Lamb and his followers. John is telling the Christians to pick one side or the other. The Christians were tempted to try to compromise, to live with one foot in each camp. John uses stark language in these chapters to show that this is no longer an option. Finally the Christians have to choose where they give their ultimate allegiance.

The issue that John raises here is still important for modern day Christians. Twenty-first century American Christians, perhaps even more than first century Asian Christians, are tempted to live with one foot in American culture and one foot in Christianity. John is telling us that is not always possible.

I learned the truth of this in the first congregation that I served as pastor. I served a church in a small city in Kentucky in the early 1980s. I think it safe to say that my members wanted to live both as good citizens of the town and as Christians. The town at the time was quite segregated. At high school basketball games, there was a black section and a white section. There were three funeral homes in town, one for blacks and two for whites. The churches were also segregated. Blacks and whites did not worship together.

One summer we offered Vacation Bible School and we advertised in the local newspaper. A couple of black families saw the ad and asked if they could send their children. As pastor I said sure. That created quite a bit of concern in the community. Some of our church members thought it inappropriate to have blacks in the church. Other people around town made it clear that blacks should not be attending Vacation Bible School at a white congregation.

The congregation struggled with the issue and decided that all children were welcome. We included the black children and even had some black families join us for the closing worship. But what the congregation and I had to struggle with was that on this issue we could no longer be good citizens of the town and Christians. We had to pick a side. The rules of the town were clear—no blacks in white churches. Jesus was also clear—all people are invited to his church. The congregation was faced with an issue that placed following Jesus in conflict with the prevailing norms of the community. The congregation had to choose. I have to say I'm proud of the congregation, as they did the right thing.

This is the sort of issue that John raises for us. Whose side will we ultimately be on? Sometimes our culture conforms to Christian values, or at least is not in conflict with the teachings of Christ. But there will be times when being faithful to Jesus will put us at odds with the values of our culture, and we will need to decide where our ultimate allegiance lies. The challenge of the book of Revelation is to dare to be faithful to Jesus, no matter what.

14:14-20

¹⁴Then I looked, and there was a white cloud, and seated on the cloud was one like the Son of Man, with a golden crown on his head, and a sharp sickle in his hand! ¹⁵Another angel came out of the temple, calling with a loud voice to the one who sat on the cloud, "Use your sickle and reap, for the hour to reap has come, because the harvest of the earth is fully ripe." ¹⁶So the one who sat on the cloud swung his sickle over the earth, and the earth was reaped.

¹⁷Then another angel came out of the temple in heaven, and he too had a sharp sickle. ¹⁸Then another angel came out from the altar, the angel who has authority over fire, and he called with a loud voice to him who had the sharp sickle, "Use your sharp sickle and gather the clusters of the vine of the earth, for its grapes are ripe." ¹⁹So the angel swung his sickle over the earth and gathered the vintage of the earth, and he threw it into the great wine press of the wrath of God. ²⁰And the wine press was trodden outside the city, and blood flowed from the wine press, as high as a horse's bridle, for a distance of about two hundred miles.

John now continues this theme of picking a side and he does so by showing us the results of our picking. For those who choose God there is salvation. For those who choose Satan, there is judgment.

Verses 14-16 speak of a harvest. A grain harvest in the Bible is often positive imagery for bringing in the kingdom of God. (For example, Mark 4:29 or Matt 9:37-38.) In this section one "like the Son of Man with a golden crown on his head" comes and harvests. This figure is Jesus, and the harvest refers to the ingathering of the faithful. (Note how this image ties in with the image of the "first fruits" in verse 4 of this chapter.) This harvesting is an image of salvation for the faithful.

Verses 17-20 speak of a reaping. But this imagery is one of judgment and wrath. The reaping refers to the judgment of those who are not faithful to Jesus. The imagery is horrid (blood flowing "as high as a horse's bridle") as we are warned of the seriousness of ignoring Jesus.

John in chapter 14 has been calling for people to pick a side, to make a choice. In these final verses he shows the results of that choice. For those who follow the Lamb, there is salvation. For those who follow the ways of the world, there will be judgment.

Section IX
Seven Bowls of Wrath

Chapters 15–16

In this section we return again to a series of judgments. There have been seven seals and seven trumpets. Now come seven bowls of the wrath of God. There is one difference this time, as we are alerted that these "are the last, for with them the wrath of God is ended" (15:1). Continue to watch how judgment in Revelation is meant to serve the goal of redemption, as God's deepest desire is to save all people.

Chapter 15

15:1-8

Then I saw another portent in heaven, great and amazing: seven angels with seven plagues, which are the last, for with them the wrath of God is ended.

²And I saw what appeared to be a sea of glass mixed with fire, and those who had conquered the beast and its image and the number of its name, standing beside the sea of glass with harps of God in their hands. ³And they sing the song of Moses, the servant of God, and the song of the Lamb: "Great and amazing are your deeds, Lord God the Almighty! Just and true are your ways, King of the nations! ⁴Lord, who will not fear and glorify your name? For you alone are holy. All nations will come and worship before you, for your judgments have been revealed."

⁵After this I looked, and the temple of the tent of witness in heaven was opened, ⁶and out of the temple came the seven angels with the seven plagues, robed in pure bright linen, with golden sashes across their chests. ⁷Then one of the four living creatures gave the seven angels seven golden bowls full of the wrath of God, who lives forever and ever; ⁸and the temple was filled with smoke from the glory of God and from his power, and no one could enter the temple until the seven plagues of the seven angels were ended.

John now sees another sign in heaven, seven angels with seven plagues. This is reminiscent of 8:2, where he sees seven angels with seven trumpets. But this time the reading announces that these plagues will be the last.

John next sees a "sea of glass mixed with fire" and those who had conquered the beast standing by the sea. We do well to let our imaginations play with the image of a sea of glass mixed with fire. What in the world would this look like? Once again John stretches our imaginations! Back in chapter 4, John described the heavenly throne room and mentioned a sea of glass before the throne of God. Here he makes use of that imagery again.

The conquerors, those who have overcome the beast, gather by this heavenly sea and sing a song of praise to God. This scene recalls the Old Testament story of the deliverance of the Israelites from the Egyptians at the Red Sea. In Exodus 15, after the Israelites are delivered, Moses and the people stand by the sea and sing a song of victory. Now in this heavenly scene, the conquerors sing the song of Moses and the song of the Lamb. Like the ancient people of Israel, they celebrate their deliverance, particularly the deliverance that is now given in Jesus Christ.

Two comments on this song and imagery are appropriate. First, John once again draws from the Exodus story, for the Exodus story provides a good framework for understanding the judgment of God. In Revelation, as in Exodus, judgment serves the purpose of redemption and liberation.

Second, verse 4 in the song proclaims, "All nations will come and worship before you." This is God's will. Revelation is not just a book of divine vengeance. Quite the contrary, Revelation portrays God's deepest desire as being the redemption of all people and all nations. That purpose is restated here. God is out to save the nations!

John next sees "the temple of the tent of witness in heaven." (This again refers to the Exodus story. In Exodus 25:9, while Moses is on Mt. Sinai, God shows Moses the heavenly tent of witness or tabernacle. The people of Israel then make a tabernacle based on that.) This heavenly temple is opened, and out come seven angels dressed in bright linen robes and golden sashes. John's descriptive language is clear—this is a liturgical procession! The angels are given seven bowls filled with the wrath of God. The temple then fills with smoke. This smoke serves two purposes. First, it emphasizes the glory of God. Second, it announces that there is no turning back until these plagues are finished.

Points to Ponder

1. We've been saying that Revelation is a spiral of visions, with repetitions and enhancing of themes. We now begin another spiral. There have been the seven seals and the seven trumpets. Now we come to another series of judgment, the seven bowls of the wrath of God.

2. Revelation in chapter 15 has returned once again to worship. That is central for the book. Revelation is grounded in and continually returns to worship.

Chapter 16

16:1-9

Then I heard a loud voice from the temple telling the seven angels, "Go and pour out on the earth the seven bowls of the wrath of God." ²So the first angel went and poured his bowl on the earth, and a foul and painful sore came on those who had the mark of the beast and who worshiped its image. [3]The second angel poured his bowl into the sea, and it became like the blood of a corpse, and every living thing in the sea died.

[4]The third angel poured his bowl into the rivers and the springs of water, and they became blood. [5]And I heard the angel of the waters say, "You are just, O Holy One, who are and were, for you have judged these things; [6]because they shed the blood of saints and prophets, you have given them blood to drink. It is what they deserve!" [7]And I heard the altar respond, "Yes, O Lord God, the Almighty, your judgments are true and just!"

[8]The fourth angel poured his bowl on the sun, and it was allowed to scorch them with fire; [9]they were scorched by the fierce heat, but they cursed the name of God, who had authority over these plagues, and they did not repent and give him glory.

We now begin this new and final series of plagues. A loud voice instructs the angels to pour their bowls on the earth. One by one the angels do just that.

The first angel pours his bowl and a "foul and painful sore" comes on all who have the mark of the beast. The affliction here is not on humankind in general; it is directed to those who follow the beast. There is a specific word of judgment in this section on Rome and on those who follow the ways of Rome. Plagues one, five, six, and seven are all directed to Rome and its followers. We also do well to note that this plague, like so many of the plagues in Revelation, is rooted in the plagues on Egypt in the Exodus story. This first bowl echoes Exodus 9:10-11 and the sores that came on the Egyptian people.

The second angel pours his bowl into the sea, and the sea becomes like the blood of a corpse. This is horrid imagery! Every living thing in the sea dies. Once again we have an echo of the plagues on Egypt, that of water being turned into blood (Exod 7:17-21).

The third angel pours his bowl on the rivers and the springs of water. Now the fresh waters become like blood. Again we have an echo of the plague on Egypt. The angel then in verses 5 and 6 stops and makes a point to proclaim the justice of God ("You are just, O Holy One"). It is as if, in the midst of all the judgment, we need to be reminded that God's judgments are not arbitrary, but just and right as he reclaims his fallen creation. We also do well in these verses to see the restraint of God.[1] We

[1] Craig Koester, *Revelation and the End of All Things* (Grand Rapids: Wm. Eerdmans Publishing Company, 2001), 150.

usually don't think of Revelation in terms of restraint. But that is the case here. Those who are being judged have shed the blood of the saints. You would think that retribution would demand that these people would have their own blood shed. But now, rather than having their blood shed, they are given blood to drink. As harsh as the judgment is, it is less than the offense.

The fourth angel pours his bowl on the sun and it scorches God's opponents with heat. This bowl does not have a counterpart in the Exodus story. There is rather a contrast here with 7:16. In 7:16, those who have conquered are promised that "the sun will not strike them, nor any scorching heat." Here those who have opposed God are scorched by the sun. Perhaps the most significant thing in this paragraph is the response of those who are scorched. As is so often the case in Revelation, those who are afflicted do not repent. Instead they respond by cursing God. Even in the face of all this judgment, the people respond by cursing rather than repenting.

16:10-11

The fifth angel poured his bowl on the throne of the beast, and its kingdom was plunged into darkness; people gnawed their tongues in agony, [11]and cursed the God of heaven because of their pains and sores, and they did not repent of their deeds.

The last three bowls of wrath are directed specifically to the beast Rome. The fifth angel pours his bowl on "the throne of the beast," and plunges the beast's kingdom into darkness. Once again we have an echo of the Exodus story, Exodus 10:21, where darkness covers the land of Egypt. The beast's kingdom is thrown into darkness and the people into agony, but once again they refuse to repent. This becomes an ongoing theme in Revelation; God's desire is the repentance of people, but people refuse again and again and again!

We also need to note how this plague, and the plagues that follow, would be heard as good news by the Christians who were threatened by Rome. For the persecuted Christians (for example, in Smyrna or Philadelphia), this word of the judgment of Rome would be heard as a word of deliverance.

16:12-16

The sixth angel poured his bowl on the great river Euphrates, and its water was dried up in order to prepare the way for the kings from the east. [13]And I saw three foul spirits like frogs coming from the mouth of the dragon, from the mouth of the beast, and from the mouth of the false prophet. [14]These are demonic spirits, performing signs, who go abroad to the kings of the whole world, to assemble them for battle on the great day of God the Almighty. [15]("See, I am coming like a thief! Blessed is the one who stays awake and is clothed, not going about naked and exposed to shame.") [16]And they assembled them at the place that in Hebrew is called Harmagedon.

The sixth angel pours his bowl and the Euphrates River is dried up in preparation for an invasion from the east. As has been the case in previous passages (6:2, 9:13ff), we hear again echoes of the fear of an invasion by the Parthian Empire. This is a word of threat, but a threat of judgment on Rome.

But in the face of this threat, evil does not give up. Instead "three foul spirits like frogs" come from the mouths of the dragon, the beast, and the false prophet.[2] (The second beast, the beast from the land, is now called the false prophet.) These demonic spirits summon and assemble the "kings of the whole world" for battle against God. In the face of God's judgment, this evil threesome does not repent. Instead they summon all the forces they can for a final stand against God.

John interrupts this line of thought in verse 15 with a comment from Jesus. In an interlude statement Jesus reminds us that he is coming like a thief, and we are to stay vigilant. We are given a reminder, right in the midst of the story, not to try to put these events on a dateline or a calendar. We do not know the time of the end, and we are here directed not to try to calculate it. (Unfortunately too many readers of Revelation ignore this instruction! Revelation has been used time and again to calculate that which we are instructed not to calculate.) Our role is rather to stay diligent in faith.

In verse 16 John returns to the flow of the story. The kings of all the earth are assembled at the place that is called Harmagedon. Evil will make its stand against God. Once again we are faced with the incredible

---

[2] This imagery of "three foul spirits like frogs" should be read as a putdown of the dragon, beast, and false prophet. The imagery suggests that what comes out of their mouths is like the croaking of frogs!

thought that in the face of all this judgment, humankind still refuses to repent. Humankind would rather fight against its Creator. We are left to wonder at just how hard the human heart is.

Armageddon

This is the only mention in the book of Revelation of Armageddon. The imagery of Armageddon has captured imaginations for centuries. We do well to ask what this imagery means.

The best translation of the Hebrew word "Armageddon" is "the mountain of Megiddo." Megiddo is a plain in northern Israel. There is a mound at the modern day locale that is being excavated. Megiddo was the site of a number of Old Testament battles. (For example, see Judges 5:19 and 2 Chronicles 35:22. Also in the Old Testament, Zechariah 12:11 speaks of Megiddo as a place where worshipers of a pagan god mourned.) The Old Testament references point to Megiddo as a place of destruction for the enemies of God.

We do well not to take this location literally. In the first place, we know from the rest of the book that John often uses geography in symbolic ways. Secondly, there is no literal "mountain of Megiddo." Megiddo is a plain. John is giving us a pointed reminder here that this is symbolic literature and is to be interpreted as such. The point here is not to locate a final battle on a map, but to proclaim that God will defeat evil! The purpose of this imagery is not to explain geography, but rather to proclaim in powerful and provocative language God's promise of hope and ultimate victory!

Having said all this, we next need to note that the final battle is not fought at this point in the book. John has a habit in Revelation of introducing concepts early in the book, and then developing and fleshing out the concept later. He does that here. The final battle is introduced here, but it is not fought. It is not until 19:19 and following that the final battle will be engaged.

16:17-21

The seventh angel poured his bowl into the air, and a loud voice came out of the temple, from the throne, saying, "It is done!" [18]And there came flashes of lightning, rumblings, peals of thunder, and a violent earthquake, such as had not occurred since people were upon the earth, so violent was that earthquake. [19]The great city was split into three parts, and the cities of the nations fell. God remembered great Babylon and gave her the wine-cup of the fury of his wrath. [20]And every island fled away, and no mountains were to be found; [21]and huge hailstones, each weighing about a hundred pounds, dropped from heaven on people, until they cursed God for the plague of the hail, so fearful was that plague.

The seventh angel pours his bowl into the air. A voice from the temple announces, "It is done!" There is lightning, thunder, a violent earthquake, huge hailstones. The great city, Babylon/Rome is split into three parts, and the cities of the nations fall. Rome is now judged and its destruction is complete. The point here is not to give exact details of the destruction of Rome, but rather to announce that the destruction is inevitable. As Caird points out, this imagery is best seen as a "political catastrophe, not a natural one."[3] The point is that Rome will be judged.

Two comments are in order on this seventh bowl. First, the judgment of Rome is here announced, but is dealt with rather briefly. John will go into much more detail about this in chapters 17 and 18. Second, this section ends with the comment that still the people curse God and do not repent. The focus is not so much on what happens to Rome, but on the question of repentance. Craig Koester has a most helpful observation on this: "Yet the comment that concludes this scene of devastation does not focus on the annihilation of the wicked, but on their refusal to repent. Rather than surrendering to God, they continue to curse God, as they have done in the face of previous plagues. The question is, will Revelation's readers do the same?"[4] Perhaps the best question to end this chapter on is not by asking about what happened to ancient Rome. Rather we should ask, will we in our lives be open to repentance and the newness of God?

[3] G. B. Caird, *A Commentary on the Revelation of Saint John the Divine* (New York: Harper & Row, 1966), 209.
[4] Koester, 153–154.

Section X
The Fall of Rome

Chapters 17:1–19:10

In chapter 16 John said that Rome will fall. Now in this section John goes into more detail. In chapters 17 and 18 John shares more of his view of Rome and the judgment that awaits her. In the opening verses of chapter 19, John writes of the heavenly celebration that comes with Rome's demise.

Chapter 17

17:1-6

Then one of the seven angels who had the seven bowls came and said to me, "Come, I will show you the judgment of the great whore who is seated on many waters, [2]with whom the kings of the earth have committed fornication, and with the wine of whose fornication the inhabitants of the earth have become drunk." [3]So he carried me away in the spirit into a wilderness, and I saw a woman sitting on a scarlet beast that was full of blasphemous names, and it had seven heads and ten horns. [4]The woman was clothed in purple and scarlet, and adorned with gold and jewels and pearls, holding in her hand a golden cup full of abominations and the impurities of her fornication; [5]and on her forehead was written a name, a mystery: "Babylon the great, mother of whores and of earth's abominations." [6]And I saw that the woman was drunk with the blood of the saints and the blood of the witnesses to Jesus. When I saw her, I was greatly amazed.

One of the angels that had the seven bowls comes to John and says that he will show John "the great whore." John is taken in the spirit into a wilderness. (In the Bible, the wilderness often functions as a place of safety for God's people. In this passage it serves as a safe vantage spot from which to see the reality of the whore.) John sees a woman and a beast.

John describes the woman as "the great whore who is seated on many waters." We will learn in this chapter that this is the city of Rome. John is again drawing on Old Testament tradition. In the Old Testament, prophets sometimes referred to cities as being prostitutes. (For example, in Ezekiel 27:3 Tyre is called a prostitute.) Also in the Old Testament, the city of Babylon was described as "seated on many waters" (Jer 51:13). The "many waters" in Jeremiah referred to Babylon's vast irrigation system. John now uses the phrase to point to Rome, with the "many waters" serving as a reference to her trading empire.[1] Rome is described as a drunken prostitute. She is dressed in purple and gold, adorned with much jewelry. In her hand is a golden cup. But the cup is filled with filth and obscenity. The woman is in a drunken stupor. Moreover the woman rides a beast, a scarlet beast with seven heads and ten horns. We know from previous chapters that the beast is the Roman Empire.

---

[1] G. B. Caird, *A Commentary on the Revelation of Saint John the Divine* (New York: Harper & Row, 1966), 213.

121

What John is doing here is writing political satire.[2] Rome was often described in terms of Roma, the mother goddess. She was the great city from which the rest of the world would orientate itself. Now John says, "Don't believe that." Rome isn't a mother or a goddess. She is a whore, a drunken whore. What John is doing is "unmasking" Rome for his readers. The Christians in places like Laodicea and Sardis were tempted to accommodate themselves to Roman ways. John here warns them not to do so, for Rome is really nothing but a prostitute. John portrays Rome so negatively that the Christians will instinctively recoil from Rome and her ways.

Note how John uses images. The people of God have been previously portrayed as a glorious woman (12:1). In chapter 19 the people of God will be portrayed as a bride. Rome is here portrayed as a prostitute. John uses stark images to help us see the true nature of things. John's intent is to unveil the ugliness of Rome in such stark terms that Christians will know to oppose her. As Caird so beautifully puts it, "The magic is broken; the fairy godmother who has put her spell on the whole world through the brilliance of her appearance and the munificence of her presents, is revealed as the old witch."[3]

17:7-18

[7]But the angel said to me, "Why are you so amazed? I will tell you the mystery of the woman, and of the beast with seven heads and ten horns that carries her. [8]The beast that you saw was, and is not, and is about to ascend from the bottomless pit and go to destruction. And the inhabitants of the earth, whose names have not been written in the book of life from the foundation of the world, will be amazed when they see the beast, because it was and is not and is to come.

[9]"This calls for a mind that has wisdom: the seven heads are seven mountains on which the woman is seated; also, they are seven kings, [10]of whom five have fallen, one is living, and the other has not yet come; and when he comes, he must remain only a little while. [11]As for the beast that was and is not, it is an eighth but it belongs to the seven, and it goes to destruction. [12]And the ten horns that you saw are ten kings who have not yet received a kingdom, but they are to receive authority as kings for one hour, together with the beast. [13]These are united in yielding their power and authority to the beast; [14]they will make war on the Lamb, and the Lamb

---

[2] Craig Koester, *Revelation and the End of All Things* (Grand Rapids: Wm. Eerdmans Publishing Company, 2001), 155 and following.
[3] Caird, 214.

> will conquer them, for he is Lord of lords and King of kings, and those
> with him are called and chosen and faithful."
>
> [15]And he said to me, "The waters that you saw, where the whore is
> seated, are peoples and multitudes and nations and languages. [16]And the
> ten horns that you saw, they and the beast will hate the whore; they will
> make her desolate and naked; they will devour her flesh and burn her up
> with fire. [17]For God has put it into their hearts to carry out his purpose by
> agreeing to give their kingdom to the beast, until the words of God will be
> fulfilled. [18]The woman you saw is the great city that rules over the kings
> of the earth."

The angel now explains the images in the previous verses. The angel
begins by describing the beast as "[it] was, and is not, and is about to ascend from the bottomless pit and go to destruction." As is often the case
in Revelation, this imagery is multilayered. In the first place, John is here,
as he did in chapter 13, drawing from the legend of Nero and particularly
the rumors of Nero's return. In the Nero legend Nero "was" because he
did live, now he "is not" because he was dead, but he is "about to ascend"
because he was rumored to be returning. In the second place John here
once again reminds us that evil parodies God—God is the one who "is
and who was and who is to come" while the beast "was, and is not, and
is about to ascend." Evil tries to make itself look like good. Third, John
makes a comment here about Roman persecution. The beast "was," meaning in the past the Roman Empire persecuted Christians. Now it "is not,"
as the persecutions were not happening. But "it will ascend" as John
foresees persecutions coming again for the Christians.

John goes on in verse 9 to write that the seven heads of the beast are
seven mountains. This is a very clear reference to Rome, the city on seven
hills. But once again John wants to use the imagery in an additional way.
He goes on to say that the seven heads are also "seven kings, of whom
five have fallen, one is living, and the other has not yet come." This is a
reference to the Roman emperors.

Some students of Revelation have thought that this passage is a place
to identify who the Roman emperor was at the time of Revelation. It
would seem logical in this passage to assume that Revelation was written
during the reign of the sixth Roman emperor. Unfortunately, it is not that
simple. We aren't sure where John would start his count, whether he
would consider Julius Caesar or Augustus the first emperor, or if he would
start with Nero, the first emperor to persecute Christians. We also don't
know if John would include the emperors who served only a short time.

This passage finally doesn't tell us who the emperor was at the time of Revelation.

As we reflect, however, perhaps we shouldn't expect this passage to tell us who the emperor was. In the first place, John's original readers knew who the emperor was. John didn't need to give them a riddle to figure that out. Moreover, in line with John's use of images, seven emperors perhaps refers to the complete line of emperors. And the eighth emperor who is a return of one of the seven seems to again play on the legend of Nero's return. Rather than using this passage to date history, we do better to see the symbolism as pointing to the full line of Roman emperors.

The angel goes on to explain that the ten horns are ten kings who receive authority and ally themselves with Rome. These kings and Rome will fight against the Lamb. But they will not succeed, for the Lamb will conquer them. Finally, and incredibly, the kings and the beast will turn on the woman! The empire and its allies will turn and destroy Rome herself!

A few comments are in order here. First, this is challenging imagery. It is a difficult section of the book. Second, we do well not to take this imagery literally. For example, do kings really rule for only one hour? Rather than pushing the imagery too literally, we do better to ask what the imagery is pointing to, which is clear. The Roman Empire and its allies will fight against the Lamb. They will not succeed. But then the Empire and its allies will turn on the whore, on Rome itself. Rome's very allies and empire will destroy her! What John is saying is that evil ultimately self-destructs. That which is opposed to God will by its very nature destroy itself. And this destruction fits the purpose of God (v. 17).

John here develops an incredible point. Rome will fall, for by its very nature evil must fail. God alone creates, and that which is opposed to God will be destructive, and will finally destroy even itself. That which is opposed to God cannot triumph and ultimately cannot survive. What an incredible message of hope, both for first century Christians and for twenty-first century Christians! No matter how bleak our world, God will triumph. We can live with the assurance of that.

John in chapter 17 is making two very clear and powerful points. First, Rome is a whore. Therefore Christians were not to accommodate themselves to Roman ways, or align themselves with Rome. Perhaps we as modern day Christians do well to ask what serves as a prostitute in our world. Are there things in our day that at a distance seem alluring and good, but at closer view reveal themselves to be harmful and evil? What seduces us away from the faith?

Second, evil will self-destruct. Rome and her allies will cave in on themselves. Likewise in our day, only that which is of God will ultimately survive. True life and final victory is found only in the Lamb who is the Lord of life.

Chapter 18

Chapter 18 continues the announcement of Rome's fall, although John now takes a different approach. Chapter 18 is basically a funeral dirge. It is an account and a lamenting of the destruction of Babylon/Rome. Watch in this chapter how the destruction of Rome is not portrayed directly. Rather, in powerful artistic fashion, John records the reactions of those who see Rome's destruction. Notice also the changing tenses in chapter 18.[4] Rome is depicted as fallen in verse 2. Then in verse 4, people are instructed to come out of her, lest they perish with Rome. This changing of tenses continues throughout the chapter. It certainly makes it difficult to try to place all of this on a calendar. John's free use of tenses reminds us that his point is not so much to give us an historical prediction, as it is to direct Christians away from the seducing power of Rome.

18:1-8

After this I saw another angel coming down from heaven, having great authority; and the earth was made bright with his splendor. [2]He called out with a mighty voice, "Fallen, fallen is Babylon the great! It has become a dwelling place of demons, a haunt of every foul spirit, a haunt of every foul and hateful bird, a haunt of every foul and hateful beast. [3]For all the nations have drunk of the wine of the wrath of her fornication, and the kings of the earth have committed fornication with her, and the merchants of the earth have grown rich from the power of her luxury."

[4]Then I heard another voice from heaven saying, "Come out of her, my people, so that you do not take part in her sins, and so that you do not share in her plagues; [5]for her sins are heaped high as heaven, and God has remembered her iniquities. [6]Render to her as she herself has rendered, and repay her double for her deeds; mix a double draught for her in the cup she mixed. [7]As she glorified herself and lived luxuriously, so give her a like measure of torment and grief. Since in her heart she says, 'I rule as a queen; I am no widow, and I will never see grief,' [8]therefore her plagues will come in a single day—pestilence and mourning and famine—and she will be burned with fire; for mighty is the Lord God who judges her."

---

[4] Koester, 162.

An angel, bright with splendor, now comes. In verses 2 and 3 the angel announces that Babylon/Rome has fallen. The language is stark, horrifying. Rome has become the dwelling place of demons, of foul birds, and hateful beasts.

In verses 4-8 another voice speaks. This voice warns, "Come out of her, my people." The language here echoes Jeremiah 51:45. The call here is not to physically move from Rome, but rather for Christians to distance themselves from the ways of Rome. Rome will be repaid for her sin, and Christians must not share in that sin.

A good question to ask at this point is, "Why is Rome being judged?" What has she done that is so sinful, so wrong? Adela Yarbro Collins provides a helpful list in her article "Revelation 18."[5] Rome will be judged for:

1. **"The idolatrous and blasphemous worship offered and encouraged by Rome, especially the emperor cult."** The fornication that John refers to in Revelation is idolatry, the worship of emperors. Worship is to be reserved only for God.
2. **"The violence perpetrated by Rome, especially against Jews and Christians."** Rome has shed the blood of Christians. We can also expand on this, based on 18:24. Not only is Rome guilty of the "blood of prophets and of saints," but also "of all who have been slaughtered on earth." Behind Roman power and glory is violence, and John condemns that.
3. **"Rome's blasphemous self-glorification."** Rome in arrogance saw herself as the center of the world. That position must be reserved for God alone.
4. **"Roman wealth."** Roman emphasis on wealth and luxuries is condemned in chapter 18.

A good question for modern day Christians to ask here is, are we guilty of any of these things? As we live in a culture that lifts up wealth, focuses on violence, and too often exhibits self-glorification and arrogance, we need to dare to ask how the book of Revelation would reshape our lives. We do well to ask how John's critique of ancient Rome speaks to our nation, to our lives, to our modern day. We too must learn, again and again, to direct our lives to God and God alone.

[5] Adela Yarbro Collins, "Revelation 18: Taunt-song or Dirge?" in Jan Lambrecht, editor, *L'Apocalypse johannique et l'apocalyptique dans le Nouveau Testament* (Gembloux: J. Duculot and Louvain: Louvain University Press, 1980) p. 203, quoted in M. Eugene Boring, *Revelation* (Louisville, Kentucky: John Knox Press, 1989), 187.

18:9-20

⁹And the kings of the earth, who committed fornication and lived in luxury with her, will weep and wail over her when they see the smoke of her burning; ¹⁰they will stand far off, in fear of her torment, and say, "Alas, alas, the great city, Babylon, the mighty city! For in one hour your judgment has come."

¹¹And the merchants of the earth weep and mourn for her, since no one buys their cargo anymore, ¹²cargo of gold, silver, jewels and pearls, fine linen, purple, silk and scarlet, all kinds of scented wood, all articles of ivory, all articles of costly wood, bronze, iron, and marble, ¹³cinnamon, spice, incense, myrrh, frankincense, wine, olive oil, choice flour and wheat, cattle and sheep, horses and chariots, slaves—and human lives. ¹⁴"The fruit for which your soul longed has gone from you, and all your dainties and your splendor are lost to you, never to be found again!" ¹⁵The merchants of these wares, who gained wealth from her, will stand far off, in fear of her torment, weeping and mourning aloud, ¹⁶"Alas, alas, the great city, clothed in fine linen, in purple and scarlet, adorned with gold, with jewels, and with pearls! ¹⁷For in one hour all this wealth has been laid waste!"

And all shipmasters and seafarers, sailors and all whose trade is on the sea, stood far off ¹⁸and cried out as they saw the smoke of her burning, "What city was like the great city?" ¹⁹And they threw dust on their heads, as they wept and mourned, crying out, "Alas, alas, the great city, where all who had ships at sea grew rich by her wealth! For in one hour she has been laid to waste. ²⁰Rejoice over her, O heaven, you saints and apostles and prophets! For God has given judgment for you against her."

Three groups now weep for Rome/Babylon: the kings of the earth, the merchants of the earth, and the shipmasters and seafarers. In verses 9 and 10 the kings who shared in Rome weep over her loss. Their grief is self-centered, as they grieve their own loss of power and wealth. In verses 14-17 the merchants of the earth grieve over the loss of Rome. As with the kings, this grief is self-centered, for the merchants have lost their source of wealth. John includes a list of luxury items that the merchants supplied for Rome. It is an incredible list, a reminder of the wealth and lavishness of Rome. The list concludes with "slaves—and human lives," as John seems to indict the Roman use of slavery. Finally in verses 17-20, the shipmasters and seafarers grieve for Rome. Once again these people are grieving as they see their source of commerce and wealth destroyed.

18:21-24

²¹Then a mighty angel took up a stone like a great millstone and threw it into the sea, saying, "With such violence Babylon the great city will be thrown down, and will be found no more; ²²and the sound of harpists and minstrels and of flutists and trumpeters will be heard in you no more; and an artisan of any trade will be found in you no more; and the sound of the millstone will be heard in you no more; ²³and the light of a lamp will shine in you no more; and the voice of bridegroom and bride will be heard in you no more; for your merchants were the magnates of the earth, and all nations were deceived by your sorcery. ²⁴And in you was found the blood of prophets and of saints, and of all who have been slaughtered on earth."

The chapter concludes with a mighty angel throwing a great millstone into the sea and announcing, "With such violence Babylon the great city will be thrown down." The angel then gives a listing of things in Rome that will be ended. Notice how John in this listing does acknowledge that there is good in the glories of Roman culture. John acknowledges "the sound of harpists and minstrels and of flutists and trumpeters." He recognizes artisans, and millstones grinding, and light, and newlyweds celebrating. As Fred Craddock so powerfully summarizes: "She (Rome) has fallen, to be sure, but the poet walks among her ruins feeling the weight of the loss and singing God's victory with a heavy heart."[6]

Chapter 19

The scene now shifts from earth to heaven. On earth (chapter 18) people are mourning the fall of Rome. But in heaven (chapter 19) there is joy and celebration over the event. John continues to write about Rome's demise, but now it is from the perspective of heaven. And in heaven there is rejoicing!

19:1-5

After this I heard what seemed to be the loud voice of a great multitude in heaven, saying, "Hallelujah! Salvation and glory and power to our God, ²for his judgments are true and just; he has judged the great whore who corrupted the earth with her fornication, and he has avenged on her the blood of his servants." ³Once more they said, "Hallelujah! The smoke goes up from her forever and ever." ⁴And the twenty-four elders and the four

---

[6] Fred B. Craddock, "Preaching the Book of Revelation," *Interpretation*, 40 (1986), 277.

> living creatures fell down and worshiped God who is seated on the throne, saying, "Amen. Hallelujah!" [5]And from the throne came a voice saying, "Praise our God, all you his servants, and all who fear him, small and great."

John hears a great multitude in heaven. They are singing, "Hallelujah!" which means, "Praise the Lord!" The multitude proclaims, "Hallelujah! Salvation and glory and power to our God." This sounds like the Hallelujah Chorus from the great musical work *The Messiah*. And in fact the Hallelujah Chorus is based on Revelation 19. The heavenly multitude celebrates the fall of Rome.

Verse 2 points out that the judgment of Rome has served the cause of God's redemption. "The great whore," namely Rome, has corrupted the earth. But now she has been judged and the earth is in the process of being set free. Verses 4 and 5 continue the celebration as the heavenly court joins in to praise God and celebrate the fall of Rome.

19:6-9

> [6]Then I heard what seemed to be the voice of a great multitude, like the sound of many waters and like the sound of mighty thunderpeals, crying out, "Hallelujah! For the Lord our God the Almighty reigns. [7]Let us rejoice and exult and give him the glory, for the marriage of the Lamb has come, and his bride has made herself ready; [8]to her it has been granted to be clothed with fine linen, bright and pure"—for the fine linen is the righteous deeds of the saints. [9]And the angel said to me, "Write this: Blessed are those who are invited to the marriage supper of the Lamb." And he said to me, "These are true words of God."

The multitude continues to praise God. Then, in a new thought, the multitude announces that it is time for the marriage of the Lamb. The multitude goes on to say that the bride is ready. The announcement is of a marriage with Jesus the Lamb as groom and the people of God as bride. This image of God being the groom and the people of God being the bride is drawn from the Old Testament (for example, Isa 62:5, Jer 22, Hos 2:19-20). In fact other New Testament passages also talk about Jesus being the groom and the church the bride (for example, 2 Cor 11:2). The image of marriage serves to announce the final victory of God. Jesus and his people are now to be united in ultimate glory and salvation.

We might expect this to be the end of the book. The bride is ready, we expect that Jesus will return as groom, and the marriage feast will mark the end of the world. But by this point in Revelation we also know that John does not follow our expectations! The marriage is here announced, but it will not actually come until chapter 21. John still has many things to tell us before he gets to the final promises at the end.

Two additional points need to be made on this section. First, we do well to pay attention to the stark contrast that John has developed. Rome is a whore (17:1), a whore that bought and coveted fine linen (18:12). The people of God are a bride, clothed in fine linen (19:8). John is again developing a stark contrast to make the Christians recoil from Rome. Second, John adds a beatitude here, "Blessed are those who are invited to the marriage supper of the Lamb." He will make further use of this image of a supper in verse 21 of this chapter.

19:10

Then I fell down at his feet to worship him, but he said to me, "You must not do that! I am a fellow servant with you and your comrades who hold the testimony of Jesus. Worship God! For the testimony of Jesus is the spirit of prophecy."

John finishes this section by sharing an odd little incident. John falls at the feet of the angel who has shown him these things and seeks to worship the angel. The angel instructs John to only worship God. There is an important point in this little incident, that we are to worship God and only God. Even other good things (such as angels!) cannot take God's place as the object of worship.

The verse concludes with an important statement about the nature of prophecy: "For the testimony of Jesus is the spirit of prophecy." As we have previously pointed out, for John prophecy is not simply a matter of foretelling the future. It is not about laying out a roadmap to the future. For John, prophecy is about pointing people to Jesus. The function of prophecy is to lead people into a true worshiping and following of the one Lord.

Section XI
Pictures of the End

Chapters 19:11–20:15

With 19:11 we begin a new section in the book. John will now give us seven pictures of the end of the world and the coming of the Kingdom. (John has used "sevens" as an ongoing way of organizing his work. There have been seven seals, seven trumpets, seven bowls of wrath. Now as John writes of the end he will give us another "seven," this time seven pictures.) Each of these pictures proclaims various aspects of the end. Sometimes the pictures overlap, and John doesn't seem to be particularly interested in maintaining a tight chronological sequence. But through the seven pictures he loudly and clearly proclaims God's victory. The seven pictures are: the coming of Christ, the last battle, the binding of Satan, the thousand-year reign, the defeat of Gog and Magog, the final judgment, and the coming of the new Jerusalem.

M. Eugene Boring makes a helpful observation on how to deal with this material. Boring suggests that we should see this section as an "art gallery" with "seven different pictures," with "each picture complete in itself with its own message."[1] John has given us seven different views of aspects of the end, and we do well to look carefully at each.

---

[1] M. Eugene Boring, *Revelation* (Louisville: John Knox, 1989), 195.

> **19:11-16**
>
> [11]Then I saw heaven opened, and there was a white horse! Its rider is called Faithful and True, and in righteousness he judges and makes war. [12]His eyes are like a flame of fire, and on his head are many diadems; and he has a name inscribed that no one knows but himself. [13]He is clothed in a robe dipped in blood, and his name is called The Word of God. [14]And the armies of heaven, wearing fine linen, white and pure, were following him on white horses. [15]From his mouth comes a sharp sword with which to strike down the nations, and he will rule them with a rod of iron; he will tread the wine press of the fury of the wrath of God the Almighty. [16]On his robe and on his thigh he has a name inscribed, "King of kings and Lord of lords."

A rider on a white horse appears. It is Jesus! He is described as "Faithful and True," and as the one who judges in righteousness. His eyes are like a flame of fire, and he wears many diadems, symbols of power. He also has a name that "no one knows but himself." In biblical thought, to know the name is to have access to the person. This unknown name reminds us that we do not know all there is to know about Jesus. The full mystery and wonder of the Son of God is beyond our comprehension.

Jesus' robe is dipped in blood. This echoes Isaiah 63:2-4. But the amazing thing is that it is Jesus' own blood. This is not the blood of conquered enemies. The wonder of Jesus is that he is marked by his own blood, blood that he has shed for us!

Jesus is followed by "the armies of heaven," who are dressed in white and who are also riding white horses. From Jesus' mouth comes a sharp sword. This is the same image as in 1:16, and again the sword symbolizes the Word of God. Jesus is also said to rule with a rod of iron, an image previously used in 2:27 and 12:5. This once again is an echo of Psalm 2 and a reminder that Jesus is the Messiah promised by the Old Testament. And finally, if there is still any doubt as to the identity of this rider, John further identifies him as "King of kings and Lord of lords." This is the ruling Christ, returning as he has promised!

19:17-21

[17]Then I saw an angel standing in the sun, and with a loud voice he called to all the birds that fly in midheaven, "Come, gather for the great supper of God, [18]to eat the flesh of kings, the flesh of captains, the flesh of the mighty, the flesh of horses and their riders—flesh of all, both free and slave, both small and great." [19]Then I saw the beast and the kings of the earth with their armies gathered to make war against the rider on the horse and against his army. [20]And the beast was captured, and with it the false prophet who had performed in its presence the signs by which he deceived those who had received the mark of the beast and those who worshiped its image. These two were thrown alive into the lake of fire that burns with sulfur. [21]And the rest were killed by the sword of the rider on the horse, the sword that came from his mouth; and all the birds were gorged with their flesh.

The beast and the kings of the earth now gather to battle with the rider on the white horse (Jesus). This is the battle that was announced in 16:14-16. This is Armageddon, and here it is finally fought. We do well to carefully note the details of the battle. In much of popular literature, Armageddon is portrayed as a nuclear holocaust, or as the desolation of the earth. Often in modern portrayals, there are cruise missiles, nuclear bombs, tanks, etc. But that is not what John writes. In John's battle, there is only one weapon and that is the Word of God ("the sword that came from his mouth"). In John's view, it really isn't much of a battle. The beast and the kings of the earth and their armies are gathered to make war on Jesus. But Jesus, by the power of his Word, destroys them. The battle is quick and one-sided. What John seeks to say in this imagery is that Jesus, by the power of his Word, overcomes evil. Or to put this another way, the point of this Armageddon imagery is not the *prediction* of a nuclear holocaust. It is rather the *promise* that Jesus by the power of his Word will overcome evil. This is meant to be a message of reassurance for Christians that Jesus does indeed triumph, and we can live with confidence in that.

John continues by telling us that the beast and the false prophet are thrown into the lake of fire. This is the end of them. The followers of the beast are killed, and the birds eat their flesh. A few comments are in order on this imagery of the birds eating flesh. First, this imagery is drawn from Ezekiel 39:17-20. John is once again using the Old Testament. Second, this is grotesque imagery! The birds of the air eat the flesh of the followers of the beast. And even more, in verse 17 this is described as "the great supper of God." Third, what John is doing here is lifting up a contrast between two meals. John has already introduced the "marriage supper of the Lamb" back in verse 9 of this chapter. Now he introduces this second supper, of birds gorging themselves on human flesh. John is not so subtly asking the Christians which supper they would like to attend. The Christians, and all people, will attend one supper or the other. Which will it be? The imagery is stark, harsh. But John is doing here what he has already done in chapters 13 and 14. John is again setting up a stark contrast and telling people to either pick Jesus' side or Rome's side. There is no middle ground.

A final thought: as we read Revelation, we sometimes recoil against these images of Jesus going to war, and this imagery of birds eating flesh. But the final point in all this is that Jesus will and must finally defeat evil. Evil has been given every opportunity to repent. But when evil refuses to repent, it must be destroyed as God redeems his creation.

Chapter 20

We now come to a portion of Revelation that is called the millennium. The millennium refers to the thousand-year period when Satan is bound, and some people are raised to reign with Christ. These next passages have historically sparked more arguments than any other in the book. As G. B. Caird writes, "We come now to a passage which, more than any other in the book, has been the paradise of cranks and fanatics on the one hand, and literalists on the other."[2]

These next portions are brief, sparse accounts for John, but they have given rise to all sorts of arguments about their interpretation. There have been massive arguments between a premillennial position (Jesus comes first, then the thousand-year period) and a postmillennial position (there is a thousand years of improvement, which ends with the coming of Christ.)[3] Rather than raising these arguments again, let's look at what John writes. We begin with the picture of Satan being bound (vv. 1-3), and then follow with the picture of the thousand-year reign (vv. 4-6).

---

[2] G. B. Caird, *A Commentary on the Revelation of Saint John the Divine* (New York: Harper & Row, 1966), 249.

[3] For a helpful treatment of pre and postmillennial positions, see *Word & World: Theology for Christian Ministry* magazine, Volume XV, Spring 1995. There are two helpful articles: *On the Verge of the Millennium: A History of the Interpretation of Revelation* by Craig Koester, p. 128, and *The Future in Our Past: Post-millennialism in American Protestantism* by Nancy Koester, p. 137.

20:1-3

Then I saw an angel coming down from heaven, holding in his hand the key to the bottomless pit and a great chain. [2]He seized the dragon, that ancient serpent, who is the Devil and Satan, and bound him for a thousand years, [3]and threw him into the pit, and locked and sealed it over him, so that he would deceive the nations no more, until the thousand years were ended. After that he must be let out for a little while.

An angel comes. The dragon/Satan is seized, bound, and locked in the bottomless pit for a thousand years. It is helpful here to see the "progressive defeat" of Satan. In chapter 12, Satan is kicked out of heaven. In chapter 19 Satan's allies, the beast and false prophet, are thrown into the lake of fire. Now in chapter 20, Satan is first locked up for a thousand years, then is finally thrown into the lake of fire. Notice that Satan does not change after any of his defeats. Craig Koester has a helpful comment here. "The pattern shows that Satan does not change or compromise. Therefore, those who encounter his power must resist it without compromise, confident that God Himself will not compromise, but will finally bring Satan's rampage to an end."[4]

Satan is locked in the bottomless pit for a thousand years. But the passage ends with an ominous note: "after that he must be let out for a little while."

20:4-6

[4]Then I saw thrones, and those seated on them were given authority to judge. I also saw the souls of those who had been beheaded for their testimony to Jesus and for the word of God. They had not worshipped the beast or its image and had not received its mark on their foreheads or their hands. They came to life and reigned with Christ a thousand years. [5](The rest of the dead did not come to life until the thousand years were ended.) This is the first resurrection. [6]Blessed and holy are those who share in the first resurrection. Over these the second death has no power, but they will be priests of God and of Christ, and they will reign with him a thousand years.

John next sees thrones, and writes that those seated on the thrones are given authority to judge. He also sees martyrs, those beheaded for

---

[4] Craig Koester, *Revelation and the End of All Things* (Grand Rapids: Wm. Eerdmans Publishing Company, 2001), 188.

Christ. The martyrs are raised and allowed to reign with Christ for a thousand years. We need to be a bit careful at this point. It is usually assumed that those seated on the thrones are the martyrs, and that certainly is a possible reading. But the text itself is ambiguous. It just isn't clear if those on the thrones are the same as the martyrs.[5] Most likely they are, but we need to recognize the ambiguity in the reading.

John calls this raising of the dead "the first resurrection." John divides the resurrection into two parts. The first resurrection refers to these people who are here raised to reign for a thousand years. The second part of the resurrection will occur, according to John, after the thousand years when all the rest of humankind is raised to stand before the throne of God (vv. 11-15). In this "second resurrection," some will be sent to judgment, some to salvation. When John uses the term "second death," he is referring to those in the second resurrection who are subject to judgment. We also do well to note that Revelation is the only New Testament book that refers to the resurrection in phases like this.

Once again, this thousand-year period when Satan is bound and these people reign with Christ is called the millennium. However, is this meant to describe a literal thousand-year time period? Koester has a helpful insight. We know not to take the spatial references in this imagery literally. For example, no one asks where on the globe the opening to the bottomless pit is. Likewise, we do well not to take the references to time literally. As Koester points out, "John uses physical and spatial images for spiritual realities."[6]

That leaves the question, "What is the point of all this?" The millennium does two things. First, this "first resurrection" and thousand-year reign gives a priority to those who die for the faith. In effect this passage answers the question that was asked in 6:10. Back in 6:10, when the fifth seal was opened, the question was raised, what about those who are martyred for the faith? This section assures us that God has not forgotten the martyrs. On the contrary, there is something special prepared for them, namely this thousand-year reign.

Second, this passage also helps to develop the idea of the resilience of evil. Satan is stopped for a thousand years, yet he will come back. Evil is incredibly resilient. This idea will be developed more in the next section.

---

[5] By way of possibility, perhaps those on the thrones are the elders who were mentioned in 4:4, or perhaps a greater group of Christians that also included faithful people who had not been martyred.

[6] Koester, *Revelation and the End of All Things,* 181.

20:7-10

⁷When the thousand years are ended, Satan will be released from his prison ⁸and will come out to deceive the nations at the four corners of the earth, Gog and Magog, in order to gather them for battle; they are as numerous as the sands of the sea. ⁹They marched up over the breadth of the earth and surrounded the camp of the saints and the beloved city. And fire came down from heaven and consumed them. ¹⁰And the devil who had deceived them was thrown into the lake of fire and sulfur, where the beast and the false prophet were, and they will be tormented day and night forever and ever.

When the thousand years is completed, Satan is released from prison. He immediately gathers allies to attack the Christians. Satan gathers and leads the nations, identified here as Gog and Magog, against the saints. The names Gog and Magog are taken from Ezekiel 38–39. In Ezekiel, Gog is a prince from the land of Magog who will invade Israel. Gog is said to invade during a time of security. The story is a warning for Israel to stay alert. John now reinterprets this story and says that nations identified as Gog and Magog will attack God's people. Satan rallies these nations, and they "surrounded the camp of the saints and the beloved city."

However, the battle is brief. Fire comes down from heaven and destroys the enemies. Now the devil is once and for all thrown into the lake of fire. Finally, Satan is brought to an end.

This story raises a number of issues. First, will Satan ever learn? He has been defeated in heaven (ch. 12). His allies, the beast and false prophet, have been destroyed (ch. 19). Satan himself has just served a thousand-year prison term. You would think that Satan would learn to straighten up. But this story points out that Satan does not learn and will never repent. The point of this is a warning for Christians to be vigilant against Satan. First century Christians and twenty-first century Christians need to watch out for Satan, for he will not change.

A second and more pointed question is, "How does Satan find any allies to lead against the saints?" Satan has just been imprisoned for a thousand years. You would envision that as a period of peace and prosperity and faithfulness. But now as soon as Satan is released, he immediately finds allies. You have to ask, who is left to follow Satan, or why would anyone want to follow Satan at this time? John doesn't answer this question, but perhaps this story is meant to evoke astonishment in us.[7] As incredible as it seems, whenever Satan is active, people will follow him!

Third, this story reminds us that evil keeps coming back, even when we think it is destroyed. Unfortunately, human history bears witness to this all too well.

Fourth, notice how the Christians' location is described as a camp. Until the new heaven and new earth come, Christians are always on a journey.

Finally, this story reminds us that it is ultimately not enough to restrain evil.[8] It finally must be destroyed as God brings about his new creation. When evil will not repent, it must be overcome.

20:11-15

[11]Then I saw a great white throne and the one who sat on it; the earth and the heaven fled from his presence, and no place was found for them. [12]And I saw the dead, great and small, standing before the throne, and books were opened. Also another book was opened, the book of life. And the dead were judged according to their works, as recorded in the books. [13]And the sea gave up the dead that were in it, Death and Hades gave up the dead that were in them, and all were judged according to what they had done. [14]Then Death and Hades were thrown into the lake of fire. This is the second death, the lake of fire; [15]and anyone whose name was not found written in the book of life was thrown into the lake of fire.

A great white throne now appears, and the one who sits on it. This is God himself! Earth and heaven flee from his presence. The old earth and heaven flee before the moral grandeur of God.[9]

Now all people, great and small, stand before God. We do well to reflect on what John is saying here. The time will come when each of us will stand before God and account for our lives. We are responsible to our Creator. That realization ought to shape how we live.

John goes on to say that two sets of books are opened. The first set is the book of deeds. This is an accounting of all that the dead who are now raised have done. This first set of books reminds us that we are accountable for our actions. The second set is the book of life. This is a listing of those who belong to the Lamb. It is a book of divine grace, of those saved in Jesus. John paints a picture with two sets of books to resolve

---

[7] Koesler, 188.

[8] Ibid.

[9] Caird, 258.

an age-old issue in the faith. As Christians we need to say two things. First is that we are saved by grace. We do not earn salvation; it is given us in Christ as divine gift. Second, we are nonetheless accountable for our deeds. Biblically we have to say both of these things. Christians have struggled for hundreds of years with how to affirm both. John does so by painting a picture with two sets of books that are to be opened on the judgment day. In doing so he lifts up both divine grace and human responsibility. John is also careful to point out (v. 15) that we are finally saved by grace, i.e., by having our names written in the book of life.

This section closes as Death and Hades are now destroyed, thrown into the lake of fire. Likewise those who do not belong to Christ are thrown into the lake of fire. This judgment is identified as the second death. All that is opposed to God has now been dealt with and the stage is set for the coming of the new creation.

Section XII
The New Jerusalem
Chapters 21:1–22:5

As we begin chapter 21, we come to the new heaven and the new earth. It has been a long journey, but we have made it, and John has an incredible message of what is in store for God's people! Listen for how the promises keep coming and coming and coming. John presents a magnificent picture of hope and joy!

Chapter 21

21:1-8

Then I saw a new heaven and a new earth; for the first heaven and the first earth had passed away, and the sea was no more. [2]And I saw the holy city, the new Jerusalem, coming down out of heaven from God, prepared as a bride adorned for her husband. [3]And I heard a loud voice from the throne saying, "See, the home of God is among mortals. He will dwell with them as their God; and they will be his peoples, and God himself will be with them; [4]he will wipe every tear from their eyes. Death will be no more; mourning and crying and pain will be no more, for the first things have passed away."

[5]And the one who was seated on the throne said, "See, I am making all things new." Also he said, "Write this, for these words are trustworthy and true." [6]Then he said to me, "It is done! I am the Alpha and the Omega, the beginning and the end. To the thirsty I will give water as a gift from the spring of the water of life. [7]Those who conquer will inherit these things, and I will be their God and they will be my children. [8]But as for the cowardly, the faithless, the polluted, the murderers, the fornicators, the sorcerers, the idolaters, and all liars, their place will be in the lake that burns with fire and sulfur, which is the second death."

A new heaven and new earth appear. The old heaven and earth were marred by sin and polluted by tragedy. They now pass away as the new creation comes. God in his redeeming brings about a whole new creation. John notes that in this new heaven and earth, the sea is no more. The sea in the Bible is often a symbol of chaos and of a power that God has to subdue. Now in the new creation, all chaos and opposition are gone.

John sees "the holy city, the new Jerusalem, coming down out of heaven." The place for God's people is described as a city. Salvation for John is not described as solitary people floating around on clouds. It is rather described as a city, or we might say, a community. God's will is that God's people live in community, both now and in the new creation to come.

This city comes down from heaven. The Greek wording of this phrase actually implies that the city continually comes down from heaven, an ongoing gift of God. In a magnificent mixing of metaphors, this New Jerusalem is also described as a bride adorned for her husband. The people of God (i. e. the New Jerusalem) is the bride, and is now to be united to Jesus the Lamb. Now is the marriage feast that was first announced back in chapter 19! The fullness of God's salvation has come.

Verses 3 and 4 go on to speak some of the most beautiful promises in the Bible. These are incredible promises: God will dwell with his people; God will wipe away every tear from our eyes. (Stop and think what an incredibly loving and tender God this is!) Moreover death, mourning, crying, and pain will be no more. These verses are a collage of Old Testament promises (Ezek 37:27, Zech 2:10-11 and 8:8, Isa 25:8 and 65:17, 19). We frequently use these verses from Revelation in funerals, and it is most appropriate that we do. This is a poignant proclamation of the wonder that awaits us in Jesus.

John also is true to form in his use of symbolism here. In these closing chapters, he lists seven elements from the old order that will not be included in the new creation.[1] They are: sea, death, grief, crying, pain, all that is under God's curse, and night. With the number seven we realize that all that is dark and painful will be excluded from the new creation.

In verses 5-8, God speaks. God begins by saying, "See, I am making all things new." That wording is significant. God does not say that he is making all new things.[2] God's will is not to start over with all new things, but rather to redeem and renew a sinful world. Even more, God's will is to redeem and renew sinners like us! The good news is that God makes us new.

God continues by saying, "I am the Alpha and the Omega, the beginning and the end." As Caird so powerfully points out, the end in Revelation is not an event, but a person.[3] Too often we think of the end in Revelation in terms of great cataclysmic destruction or a nuclear holocaust. That is not the case. The end in Revelation is God. In the Bible, all things begin in God and end in God. Or to put this in terms of promise, at the end we will be met by One that we already know, the God who has created us and redeemed us. We dare to look forward with confidence, for the future is the Lord God!

God goes on to say, "I will be their God and they will be my children." As Caird also points out, in the verses that follow the New Jerusalem will be described in marvelous and incredible terms. But here it

---

[1] G. B. Caird, *A Commentary on the Revelation of Saint John the Divine* (New York: Harper & Row, 1966), 262.

[2] M. Eugene Boring, *Revelation* (Louisville: John Knox, 1989), 220.

[3] Caird, 266.

is first described in terms of family, of belonging to the family of God.[4] Salvation is knowing that we are God's children.

The passage ends with a word of warning. Those who live in disobedience will not share in the victory to come. Note how the sins listed relate directly to the circumstances of the seven churches.

21:9-21

[9]Then one of the seven angels who had the seven bowls full of the seven last plagues came and said to me, "Come, I will show you the bride, the wife of the Lamb." [10]And in the spirit he carried me away to a great, high mountain and showed me the holy city Jerusalem coming down out of heaven from God. [11]It has the glory of God and a radiance like a very rare jewel, like jasper, clear as crystal. [12]It has a great, high wall with twelve gates, and at the gates twelve angels, and on the gates are inscribed the names of the twelve tribes of the Israelites; [13]on the east three gates, on the north three gates, on the south three gates, and on the west three gates. [14]And the wall of the city has twelve foundations, and on them are the twelve names of the twelve apostles of the Lamb.

[15]The angel who talked to me had a measuring rod of gold to measure the city and its gates and walls. [16]The city lies foursquare, its length the same as its width; and he measured the city with his rod, fifteen hundred miles; its length and width and height are equal. [17]He also measured its wall, one hundred forty-four cubits by human measurements, which the angel was using. [18]The wall is built of jasper, while the city is pure gold, clear as glass. [19]The foundations of the wall of the city are adorned with every jewel; the first was jasper, the second sapphire, the third agate, the fourth emerald, [20]the fifth onyx, the sixth carnelian, the seventh chrysolite, the eighth beryl, the ninth topaz, the tenth chrysoprase, the eleventh jacinth, the twelfth amethyst. [21]And the twelve gates are twelve pearls, each of the gates is a single pearl, and the street of the city is pure gold, transparent as glass.

An angel shows John the New Jerusalem, which is identified as "the bride, the wife of the Lamb." As we have mentioned before, John has developed a stark contrast between Rome and the New Jerusalem. Rome is a harlot; the New Jerusalem is a bride. John's question for the early Christians was, in which city would you like to participate? John also mentions again that the New Jerusalem is coming down out of heaven from God. As we stated regarding verse 2, the city is continually coming down, an ongoing gift of grace.

---

[4] Caird, 267.

John next describes the New Jerusalem. As we read these descriptions, we do well to see the pure glory of all this. These are incredible descriptions and incredible promises! John begins by saying the city has "the glory of God and a radiance like a very rare jewel, like jasper, clear as crystal." Try to visualize this. John is deliberately stretching our imaginations. He seeks to overwhelm us with the wonder of God and the New Jerusalem. The city also has a high wall and twelve gates. In Ezekiel 48, Ezekiel has a vision in which Jerusalem has twelve gates. However, in Ezekiel's vision, the gates are exits for the tribes of Israel to leave through, while John sees the gates as entrances for all the nations of the world.[5] John also lists the gates in a strange order—east, north, south, and west. Caird suggests that there might be an anti-zodiac argument here.[6] We know the zodiac was popular in John's time. John might be deliberately corrupting the order of the zodiac as a reminder not to take the zodiac seriously. Finally John points out that the wall of the city has twelve foundations, and on them are the names of the original apostles.

In verse 15, the angel continues the tour of the city by giving John a measuring rod of gold. John measures the city and writes that the city is foursquare, "its length the same as its width." The city is fifteen hundred miles in length, width, and height. Or better, in the original Greek the measurements are twelve thousand stadia. (Note the use of twelve, a number rich in biblical imagery.) The city is a perfect cube. Now this is impossible. How can a city be a cube? Two points need to be made here. First, John is not teaching us about architecture. He is telling us about God's kingdom. He is telling us that the kingdom will be perfect, as a cube is a symbol of perfection. Second, in the Old Testament, the Holy of Holies in the middle of the temple was described as a perfect cube (1 Kgs 6:20). The New Jerusalem will be like the Holy of Holies, the place where God is.[7]

The wall of the city is next measured and is said to be fourteen cubits, or about seventy-five yards. This is odd. A city that is fifteen hundred miles high has a wall that is only seventy-five yards high? And to push the point further, why would this city need a wall? Caird provides some helpful insights here. First, in ancient times, a wall was part of the defi-

---

[5] Caird, 271.

[6] Ibid., 271–272.

[7] In describing the city's measurements, John's imagery is quite similar to the imagery used by the Greek historian Herodotus to describe ancient Babylon. For more information on this see Caird, *A Commentary on the Revelation of Saint John the Divine,* p. 274.

nition of the city. To have a city meant having a wall.[8] Moreover, the wall does not restrict access to the city. There are twelve gates that are always open. Finally, as Caird points out, "The measurements of the city show how much John cared for symbolism and how little for mathematics."[9]

The city wall is built of jasper. The image of jasper has already been used in 4:3 to describe God. The city is further said to be pure gold, clear as glass. What an incredible and impossible image! A city cannot be built of gold, nor is gold transparent. John is once again stretching our imaginations to the breaking point to tell us of the glory of the New Jerusalem. (Imagine how incredible and glorious all this must have sounded to the early Christians in the struggling congregations of Smyrna and Philadelphia. Recognize too how glorious this sounds to our ears as we look forward to the wonder that God has in store for us!)

The description continues by noting that the foundations of the city wall are adorned with twelve precious stones. These stones correspond with the twelve stones on the breastplate of the High Priest in Exodus 28:17-20.[10] Moreover, these twelve stones were also associated in John's time with the zodiac. However, here they are listed in reverse order of the zodiac. Perhaps we again have a refutation of the importance of the zodiac.[11]

John continues his description by writing that the gates of the city are pearls: in fact each gate is a single pearl. Again this is grand, but impossible. (How could a round pearl serve as a gate?) This description has taken firm root in our popular vocabulary, as it is from this that we get the language of the "pearly gates" of heaven.

21:22-27

[22]I saw no temple in the city, for its temple is the Lord God the Almighty and the Lamb. [23]And the city has no need of sun or moon to shine on it, for the glory of God is its light, and its lamp is the Lamb. [24]The nations will walk by its light, and the kings of the earth will bring their glory into it. [25]Its gates will never be shut by day—and there will be no night there. [26]People will bring into it the glory and the honor of the nations. [27]But nothing unclean will enter it, nor anyone who practices abomination or falsehood, but only those who are written in the Lamb's book of life.

---

[8] Caird, 274.
[9] Ibid., 273.
[10] Adela Yarbro Collins, *The Apocalypse New Testament Message 22* (Collegeville, MN: Liturgical Press, 1979), 149.
[11] Ibid.

John writes that there is no temple in the city. In chapters 21 and 22, John is drawing much of his imagery from the Old Testament book of Ezekiel. Ezekiel had a vision of a restored Jerusalem, and in Ezekiel's vision, the temple is central. But for John there is no need for a temple. There will be no need for a specific place to encounter God, for God's presence will fill the New Jerusalem. Or, as John writes, God himself is the temple. Likewise there is no need for sun or moon, for the glory of God is the light.

In verse 24 and following, the nations are reintroduced. The nations are said to bring their glory and honor into the New Jerusalem. That is significant, for God's will throughout the book has been the redemption, and not the destruction, of the nations. These verses also remind us that John is not against all human civilization. On the contrary, all that is good and honorable in human civilization is brought into the New Jerusalem. John condemns what is corrupt and sinful. But he also affirms humankind's ability to create that which is good. Our labors in this world are not in vain, for that which is good will be brought into the New Jerusalem.

A question that Revelation raises is, "How many of the nations or people will be saved?" Some passages imply that the nations will be destroyed (for example, 20:8). Other passages, like this one, suggest that the nations will be redeemed. Will all the nations be destroyed, will some be saved, or will all be saved? Revelation does not answer this question for us. Perhaps it is appropriate that it does not. Revelation was written to call the nations and people to faithfulness, that they might share in the New Jerusalem. It is now an open and ongoing question as to how the nations and people will respond to God. And to move the question one step closer, how will each one of us respond to God's call in Revelation that we be faithful?

Chapter 22

22:1-5

Then the angel showed me the river of the water of life, bright as crystal, flowing from the throne of God and of the Lamb [2]through the middle of the street of the city. On either side of the river, is the tree of life with its twelve kinds of fruit, producing its fruit each month; and the leaves of the tree are for the healing of the nations. [3]Nothing accursed will be found there any more. But the throne of God and of the Lamb will be in it, and

> his servants will worship him; ⁴they will see his face, and his name will be on their foreheads. ⁵And there will be no more night; they need no light of lamp or sun, for the Lord God will be their light, and they will reign forever and ever.

The opening verses of chapter 22 continue the description of New Jerusalem. The angel continues the tour by showing John "the river of the water of life, bright as crystal, flowing from the throne of God and of the Lamb." What a powerful image of life flowing from God. The new life of God is portrayed as water that cascades from the throne, rushing and overwhelming us with the abundance of God. (Perhaps a good exercise at this point would be to stop and sing "Shall We Gather at the River" as this hymn is based on this passage!) The water flows "through the middle of the street of the city." In Greek, "street" can be either singular or plural. John might envision one long street here.

John sees the "tree of life" on either side of the river. How can a tree be on both sides of a river? Once again John's image stretches our imaginations. The imagery of a tree of life draws from the story of the Garden of Eden in Genesis.[12] Back in Genesis, sin led to humankind's losing access to the tree of life. Now what was lost in Genesis is restored, as we share in the fullness of life in God. John goes on to write that this tree of life produces twelve kinds of fruit, one kind each month. This is spectacular, and perhaps we should hear an echo of the Old Testament prophets' promises of the abundance that comes with the kingdom of God.

John next adds an incredible thought—the leaves of the tree are for the healing of the nations. This again expresses a central point in Revelation—God's deepest desire is for the healing (not the destruction) of the nations. And even more, what a beautiful promise! We live in a world of strife, of brokenness, of war, of hatred. We live in a world that screams for healing. As much as humankind tries, we can't solve our own hurt. But God will do what we so long for. God will heal the nations!

John continues this magnificent description by writing that God's servants will worship God and will have God's names on their foreheads. In the Old Testament (Exod 28:36-38) the priests had God's name on their foreheads. In the New Jerusalem all take on the privilege of bearing God's name. Moreover, John writes that we will see God's face. Way

[12] Much of the imagery in chapters 21 and 22 is drawn from two Old Testament sources—Ezekiel's vision of a restored Jerusalem and the Garden of Eden story in Genesis.

back in the book of Genesis, when sin entered the human picture, humankind was separated from God. Now in Revelation the journey back is completed, and we will see God. What could it mean to see God's face? Perhaps, as Bruce Metzger points out, it involves "being near God, knowing God, and rejoicing in God all at the same time."[13]

This vision of the New Jerusalem brings us to the very throne of God. John gives us a view of what God has in store for his people, and it is awesome!

[13] Bruce Metzger, *Breaking the Code Understanding the Book of Revelation* (Nashville: Abingdon Press, 1993), 103.

Section XIII
Epilogue

Chapter 22:6-21

Having been given a glimpse of the New Jerusalem, John returns to his own time and place. We must do the same. The book concludes with an epilogue, where Jesus assures us that he is coming soon!

Chapter 22:6-21

22:6-21

⁶And he said to me, "These words are trustworthy and true, for the Lord, the God of the spirits of the prophets, has sent his angel to show his servants what must soon take place. ⁷See, I am coming soon! Blessed is the one who keeps the words of the prophecy of this book."

⁸I, John, am the one who heard and saw these things. And when I heard and saw them, I fell down to worship at the feet of the angel who showed them to me; ⁹but he said to me, "You must not do that! I am a fellow servant with you and your comrades the prophets, and with those who keep the words of this book. Worship God!"

¹⁰And he said to me, "Do not seal up the words of the prophecy of this book, for the time is near. ¹¹Let the evildoer still do evil, and the filthy still be filthy, and the righteous still do right, and the holy still be holy."

¹²"See, I am coming soon; my reward is with me, to repay according to everyone's work. ¹³I am the Alpha and the Omega, the first and the last, the beginning and the end."

¹⁴Blessed are those who wash their robes, so that they will have the right to the tree of life and may enter the city by the gates. ¹⁵Outside are the dogs and sorcerers and fornicators and murderers and idolaters, and everyone who loves and practices falsehood.

¹⁶"It is I, Jesus, who sent my angel to you with this testimony for the churches. I am the root and the descendant of David, the bright morning star."

¹⁷The Spirit and the bride say, "Come." And let everyone who hears say, "Come." And let everyone who is thirsty come. Let anyone who wishes take the water of life as a gift.

¹⁸I warn everyone who hears the words of the prophecy of this book: if anyone adds to them, God will add to that person the plagues described in this book; ¹⁹if anyone takes away from the words of the book of this prophecy, God will take away that person's share in the tree of life and in the holy city, which are described in this book.

²⁰The one who testifies to these things says, "Surely I am coming soon."

Amen. Come, Lord Jesus!

²¹The grace of the Lord Jesus be with all the saints. Amen.

Now the grandeur ends. The visions are concluded, and John returns to ordinary life. Jesus leaves John with a reminder that "these words are trustworthy and true."[1] But lest we think that all this has been just a dream, Jesus speaks again. He tells John that he is coming soon, and that we are to keep the words of the prophecy of this book. These words of Jesus in verses 6 and 7 do two things. First, they promise us that Jesus' presence does not fade away. The vision is over, but Jesus will not leave us. He is with us and is working out his purposes. Second, we are for one final time instructed on the nature of prophecy. Prophecy in Revelation is not so much about predicting the future, as about directing us to live faithfully for Jesus. That is why Jesus again tells us to keep the prophecy.

John continues in verse 8 by identifying himself as the one who heard and saw all these things. He then repeats what he did back in chapter 19 and again attempts to worship the angel. Once again John is instructed to not worship anything or anyone that is not God.

In verses 10 and 11, John is instructed not to seal up the words of the book. This is an important instruction. In the book of Daniel, specifically 12:4 and 9, Daniel is told to seal up the words of his book. The sharing of that message was to wait for a later date. John is here told just the opposite, to make this prophecy an open book for all to hear. That means that John intended for his contemporaries to hear his words. In fact John particularly directed these words to the people in the seven churches some nineteen hundred years ago. The original audience for this book was the first century Christians in Asia Minor, and these instructions in verses 10 and 11 emphasize that.

This bears pointing out, for too often modern interpreters of Revelation ignore this historical rooting. In many of the modern interpretations of Revelation, the authors assume that much of the imagery of Revelation would not be apparent until the twentieth or twenty-first century. John insists just the opposite, that his first audience was his contemporaries in first century Asia.

John continues in verse 11 by reminding us again that the time is near. He then shares a proverbial saying that basically says, "People will do what they will do, but God will work out his purposes."

"See, I am coming soon."

One question remains for us in the book of Revelation, and verse 12 raises it anew. In numerous places in the book (1:1, 1:3, 3:11, 22:6, 22:7),

---

[1] Craig Koester, *Revelation and the End of All Things* (Grand Rapids: Wm. Eerdmans Publishing Company, 2001), 201.

John writes that the time is near, or that Jesus is coming soon. That creates a problem for us as we read this nearly two thousand years after it was written. It would seem from our perspective that the time was not near, and that Jesus has not returned as soon as John indicated. How are we to understand what John is saying in these verses?

Scholars have struggled with this and have come up with a variety of answers. Here are a few:

M. Eugene Boring suggests that we simply recognize that John was wrong in this assumption.[2] Boring writes that this emphasis on coming soon was an "ingredient of apocalyptic thought," and when John chooses to write in apocalyptic fashion, he adopted this thought.[3] And, Boring writes, we need to simply acknowledge that John was wrong.[4]

G. B. Caird suggests a different approach. Caird writes that "what was coming soon" was not the end with Jesus' return, but the coming persecution.[5] Caird argues that we need to understand this urgent language not in terms of Jesus' coming, but in terms of the persecution of Christians which was soon to happen.[6]

Ardela Yarbro Collins takes a different track and writes that, "It is impossible to know what was in John's mind when he wrote those words."[7] We cannot finally determine whether John meant these words poetically or literally. But Collins adds, "It is their poetic character and their many levels of meaning that allow them still to be powerful today."[8]

Given the wide range of understandings of this issue, what do we say? Let me suggest two things. First, John, like the other authors of the New Testament, operates with a tension when he writes about the return of Jesus.[9] Some New Testament passages indicate that Christ will soon return, and Christians must be ready for that (for example, Matt 24:34). Other passages indicate that God alone knows the time when Christ will return (for example, Mark 13:32). John operates with this same tension.[10] In some passages, like 22:12, John indicates that Jesus' return is

[2] M. Eugene Boring, *Revelation* (Louisville: John Knox , 1989), 68ff.

[3] Ibid., 73.

[4] Ibid.

[5] G. B. Caird, *A Commentary on the Revelation of Saint John the Divine* (New York: Harper & Row, 1966), 236.

[6] Ibid.

[7] Adela Yarbro Collins, *The Apocalypse New Testament Message* 22 (Collegeville, MN: Liturgical Press, 1979), 153.

[8] Ibid.

[9] Koester, 203.

[10] Ibid.

imminent. In other passages, like 20:4-6, Jesus' return is at least a thousand years away. John, like the rest of the authors of the New Testament, operates with a tension when it comes to understanding the return of Jesus. This tension tells us that we ought not to try to put Jesus' return on a timeline.

Second, we do well to note how John's language functions here. When John writes that Jesus is coming soon, he is adding a note of urgency to his message. This call to discipleship and faithfulness is not something that can be delayed. Rather there is an urgency, a reality that must be addressed in the lives of Christians now!

This urgency of faith is an element of Revelation that the modern church must recover. We live in a day when Christians and the church are all too easily complacent. Too often we don't look for Christ to work in us. John reminds us that to be Christian is to live with the fire and urgency of knowing that Christ is at work now, and will come in future glory.

Let me add a final thought on this emphasis that Christ is coming soon. This thought borders on reading what was in the mind of John, and that of course is impossible. But nonetheless I think this helpful. I suspect that John would have been surprised to know that there is a twenty-first century. From his writings it seems apparent that John expected the return of Christ sooner than it has happened. And yet John, with his thorough knowledge of the Old Testament prophets, also had to know that God's timeline is never what we human beings expect. John would have been well aware that we human beings are finally not to plot out God's future activity, but are rather to live faithfully and urgently as we await the full revealing of what God will do.

Final thoughts

Revelation concludes with numerous final thoughts and reminders. Let's go through them verse by verse:

In verse 13, we are once again reminded that Jesus is the beginning and the end. We do well to note once more that this is a profound thought for Revelation. John knows that the beginning of all things is God, and the end of all things is God. The end is not described in terms of a nuclear holocaust, but in terms of Jesus. At the end we will be met by the One who even now walks with us.

Verse 14 contains the final, and seventh, beatitude in the book. Those who wash their robes in the blood of Jesus are blessed and will share in God's salvation.

Verse 15 again states that those who love falsehood and evil will not share in the New Jerusalem.

In verse 16, Jesus again points out that he is the one responsible for this testimony. Jesus describes himself as "the root and the descendant of David" and as the "bright morning star."

Verse 17 contains a beautiful invitation. Perhaps we should hear in this invitation the language of Holy Communion, and an invitation to come to the table and share in the body and blood of Jesus. If this is the case, then perhaps John envisioned this book being read in worship, and the community concluding by celebrating communion, with its promise of Jesus' coming!

Verses 18 and 19 contain a warning not to tamper with the book, and threats if people do change the reading. These verses serve as an ancient copyright to ensure that the message of the book isn't changed.[11]

John concludes the book in verses 20 and 21 with a final reminder that Jesus is coming soon. He includes a prayer that Jesus come ("Come, Lord Jesus!"), and he speaks a word of blessing for all the saints. The book ends with the assurance of Christ's presence now and the promise of Christ's return in full glory. That is the reality within which Christians live. First century Christians, and twenty-first century Christians, all of God's saints live in the grace of our Lord now, and in the assurance that he is coming.

---

[11] Bruce Metzger, *Breaking the Code: Understanding the Book of Revelation* (Nashville: Abingdon Press, 1993), 106.